THE METHODISTS OF CONTINENTAL EUROPE

THE METHODISTS OF CONTINENTAL EUROPE

BY

PAUL NEFF GARBER

Bishop of the Geneva Area of The Methodist Church

EDITORIAL DEPARTMENT
DIVISION OF EDUCATION AND CULTIVATION
GENERAL SECTION
BOARD OF MISSIONS AND CHURCH EXTENSION
THE METHODIST CHURCH
NEW YORK

Printed in the United States of America

CONTENTS

MAPS

Map of Europe, showing the countries in which Methodism has been established

PREFACE

I responded with some eagerness to the invitation to prepare a brief and popular study book on the status and historical background of Eurpean Methodism. No similar book was available on the work of the Church in this most strategic part of the world, although such work was started more than a hundred years ago.

Some false and near-slanderous statements about the Free Churches of Europe deserve to be repudiated, not by the argument of words but by the stern logic of historical facts accurately reported. Before the close of World War II a clergyman of an American denomination, historically related to one of the State-supported Churches, spent a brief period in Europe as an "observer." He visited only a few of the countries. In his printed report to the organization which sponsored his visit, this man declared that *True* the Free Churches during the war either sat on the sidelines or went over to the Nazis, while the State Churches did no such thing. As a consequence, it was asserted, the Free Churches had been discredited, while the State-subsidized groups had gained influence.

This was as far as possible from the truth. Speaking for the Methodists, who constitute the largest Free Church in many countries, I can and do categorically deny the aspersion. This point is not argued, but it is here pointed out to enable the reader to interpret the facts that will be reviewed in the light of an allegation that is both unchristian and untrue.

It is important to stress the word "continental" in the title, for this story is confined to the continent. The strong British Methodism is excluded, because the book is primarily for American Methodists and deals mainly with the groups which are organically related to the American Church. Excluded also is French North Africa, which is a part of the Geneva Area but not of the European continent.

The reader should be always aware that the writer of such a volume labors under two difficulties. The first is the inability to do justice to the subject in such a brief treatise as this. Methodism in

9

any continental nation deserves a whole volume, which could easily be filled with material of entrancing interest and high importance. It is here possible to present only the barest outline.

The second and more serious difficulty is that of writing anything today with the certainty that it will be true tomorrow. The contemporary scene in continental Europe is shifting with kaleidoscopic swiftness, and in the Soviet orbit no man knows what a day may bring forth. The reader is therefore admonished to keep the deadline of August, 1949, ever in mind.

I am particularly hopeful that the reader will give careful attention to the origins of Methodism on the continent. Uninformed persons have sometimes criticized the presence of Methodism in these countries, where Christianity and Protestantism are both old. They have seemed to believe that American Methodism launched a missionary campaign or a proselyting movement there. In point of fact, however, Methodism arose nearly everywhere under its own steam and by the preaching of nationals. In many of these countries there has never been a missionary sent out and supported by the American Church.

Dr. Elmer T. Clark, editorial secretary of the Board of Missions and Church Extension in America and the editor of the present series of study books, who knows the European situation quite well from personal contact, has written on this point: "Europe is not regarded as a 'mission field.' In most of the countries Methodism is indigenous and not the result of missionary effort, and in normal times it was self-supporting or nearly so. The European conferences are parts of The Methodist Church. The financial aid given to them is by no means comparable to the missionary appropriations made to the annual conferences in the United States. . . . Why should Methodists be there? And why should American Methodists cooperate with and help them? They actually *are* there, and not because of our initiative in most cases. They arose out of an indigenous evangelical movement and became conferences of The Methodist Church through historical circumstances. They have asked little and have received little from America, but they are parts of the Church and cannot be cast off."

Since my assignment to Europe in 1944 I have constantly gone in and out among some of the noblest and truest Christians in the world. My heart has been thrilled by their loyalty, devotion and goodness; it has been broken by the silly but brutal persecutions they have been forced to endure. Often "despised and rejected of men," even by their fellow Protestants, who feared that their principle of a Free Church freely supported by members who freely give it their allegiance, would endanger the support which others drew from governments, they have nevertheless remained steadfast and true to the evangelical faith. May God bless them every one!

Such a book as this is necessarily the product of many minds. I wish to acknowledge my deep obligation and express my sincere gratitude to the following leaders of contemporary European Methodism for their valuable assistance in the preparation of this volume: Franklin Albricias, Bishop Theodor Arvidson, Hinrich Bargmann, J. P. Bartak, Sallie Lewis Browne, Edmund Chambers, Sergei Dubrovin, R. E. E. Grob, W. H. Guiton, Ingvar Haddal, E. A. Hammarberg, Gideon Henriksson, Mansfield Hurtig, Axel Lager, Ruth Lawrence, Alf Lier, Carl Lutz, Niels Mann, Konstanty Najder, Josef Naumiuk, Eduard Raud, Antonio T. Rodriguez, Emanuele Sbaffi, George Sebele, Ferdinand Sigg, S. A. Sinisalo, Ejler Sorensen, Bishop J. W. E. Sommer, Janos Tessenyi, W. G. Thonger, Mellony Turner, Gavril Tzvetanoff, Vaclav Vancura, Vihl. Wanqvist, Werner T. Wickstrom, Ruth Wolfe, Friedrich Wunderlich. I wish also to express appreciation to my wife, Orina Kidd Garber, and to my secretary, Nina Fontana, for their helpful suggestions and constructive criticisms.

PAUL NEFF GARBER

Geneva
August, 1949

Italy, showing principal centers of Methodist work. In nearly one hundred towns are not shown there are Methodist congregations which have no buildings

CHAPTER I

METHODIST ORIGINS IN EUROPE

THERE are (1949) approximately one hundred and thirty thousand Methodists on the continent of Europe, with a constituency estimated at one-half million. There are nearly one thousand preachers who are members of Conferences, more than two thousand local preachers, and two thousand churches or preaching places. Prior to World War II the total value of Methodist properties on the continent exceeded forty million dollars.

How and when did Methodism begin in Europe? The following brief account of origins provides an answer to that question.

GERMANY

In 1810 Christopher Gottlieb Muller, a butcher, fled from Germany to England in order to escape military service under Napoleon Bonaparte. He was converted in London and became a Methodist local preacher. In 1830 he returned on a visit to his home at Winnenden, in the province of Wurttemberg, and began to preach and testify concerning his spiritual rebirth. Large audiences heard his message and he organized Sunday School classes and Methodist societies.

Muller went back to England but his converts, left without a leader, petitioned the Wesleyan Missionary Society in London to return him as a missionary. In 1831 Muller accepted the appointment, and for more than twenty years he preached in Wurttemberg and other parts of southern Germany. In 1849 he was joined by L. S. Jacoby, a German immigrant who had been converted in America.

Between 1830 and 1860 hundreds of thousands of German immigrants went to America. Some settled in the rural sections of the west while others went to such cities as Cincinnati, Louisville and St. Louis. These immigrants needed religious assistance. Although belonging nominally to the State Churches in Germany, many of them were atheists. They have been described as "sheep without a shepherd . . . living from year to year without any religious influences."

Among these German immigrants was William Nast. Under the influence of his teachers in Germany he had become an aggressive rationalist, but in America he came into contact with Methodism and resolved to become a Christian. He became a Methodist preacher and was appointed as a missionary to the German immigrants in America.

Under the leadership of Nast, who became known as the "Father of German Methodism," missions to the Germans were started in many midwestern cities. There was an annual gain of one thousand members between 1838 and 1858. By 1864 German-speaking Methodists in America were given their own annual conferences.

It was from these that a second Methodist movement went to the people of Germany. Converted Methodists in America wrote to their relatives and friends in Germany and told what Methodism had meant for them. As Dr. Paul F. Douglass, the historian of German Methodism, has said: "The strangeness of the reports in some instances turned to curiosity and curiosity in others became understanding. Letters began to come back to America from Germany asking for the kind of preachers the reports described."

Because of these requests from people in Germany, and urged by German converts in America, the Missionary Society of the Methodist Episcopal Church decided to send preachers. L. S. Jacoby, who had been born in Germany, but who in 1849 was a Methodist preacher in Illinois, was appointed as the first Methodist missionary from America to Germany. He began his ministry in Bremen in December, 1849, and he was soon joined by other preachers who went from America to participate in the Methodist revival which he started.

There was complete cooperation between Muller and Jacoby. It was agreed that Muller and his group would work in southern

Germany, while Jacoby and his associates would expand from Bremen to southern and eastern Germany. This fraternal policy led to the organic union of these two Methodist groups in Germany in 1897.

Methodism made progress in Germany despite opposition and persecution. Classes and societies were organized in many parts of the country. By 1856 the German Mission Conference was founded. This became the Germany and Switzerland Annual Conference in 1868. In 1893 there were two strong annual conferences in Germany.

SCANDINAVIA

During the nineteenth century there was a large migration of Scandinavians to America. Nearly two hundred thousand arrived in New York City between 1840 and 1876, and in addition many Scandinavian sailors landed at that port. To give spiritual and temporal care to these people, the Methodists of New York secured a ship, named it John Wesley, and transformed it into a Methodist mission. It became popularly known as the Bethel Ship. A young Swedish sailor, Olaf Gustaf Hedstrom, born in Kalmar, Sweden, who had been converted in America, became the pastor of Bethel Ship and held the first service on her deck on May 24, 1845.

The Bethel Ship became the center of Methodist work with the Scandinavians and its ministry assumed large proportions. In 1845 fifteen thousand persons attended religious services on the vessel. In 1850, Jenny Lind, the famous singer, known as the "Swedish Nightingale," was converted there and became a devout Christian. From the altar of Bethel Ship many Scandinavians went westward and along the American frontier they established Methodist societies and preached to their countrymen who had preceded them. Thus there developed in Illinois, Michigan and adjacent regions a strong Scandinavian Methodism, with its own annual conferences which maintained a separate identity until they were merged into other conferences after the unification of American Methodism.

Other Bethel Ship converts carried their newly-found faith back to Europe, and these were responsible for the rise of Methodism in

Scandinavian countries. Their letters to relatives and friends in the homeland related their spiritual experiences, and these were eagerly read and passed about. Such letters aroused strong desires to know more about the Methodist message, and the converts were implored to return and preach it. Many complied, and Methodism was born in Scandinavia, not as the result of direct foreign missionary work of the American Church, but as the reflex of the evangelism carried on from the decks of the Bethel Ship in New York.

SWEDEN

Prior to the return of Methodists from America there had been English Methodists in Sweden. British citizens desiring the pastoral care of their church petitioned the Wesleyan Missionary Society in London for a preacher. As a result J. R. Stephens went in 1826 to Stockholm and for four years preached to the English Methodists there. In 1830 George Scott succeeded Stephens, and because of his linguistic ability he began to hold Methodist services in the Swedish language. His work was so successful that by October, 1840, a Methodist church had been erected in Stockholm.

The success of Scott led to opposition by the State Church of Sweden, which by law had a monopoly on religious activity, other groups being forbidden to hold services for the Swedish people. After a riot at his church Scott was prohibited from conducting Methodist services in the Swedish language, and he went back to England in 1842.

Methodism again entered Sweden, however, by way of the Bethel Ship. John Peter Larsson was converted there, and in 1850 he returned as a layman to his native country and proclaimed the Gospel. A revival followed, and in 1854 the Missionary Society of the Methodist Episcopal Church appointed Larsson as a missionary; since he was a layman his work was not considered as a violation of the religious laws of Sweden.

The successful evangelistic meetings held by Larsson caused other Scandinavian Methodist converts to return from America. In 1865 A. Cederholm, a preacher, began to hold Methodist services on the island of Gotland, and in 1866 Victor Witting was transferred from America and became the leader at Gothenburg. Despite legal restrictions, local Methodist societies were organized, and soon Methodist chapels were erected. In 1868 the work in Sweden was organized as a separate mission, with Victor Witting as its superintendent.

In 1873 the religious laws of Sweden were liberalized for dissenters from the State Church. Other Methodist converts returned from America. Widespread evangelism ensued and a normal Methodist program gradually became possible. In 1876 the Sweden Annual Conference was organized.

NORWAY

The origin of Methodism in Norway was similar to that of Swedish Methodism. Letters from Norwegians who were converted on the Bethel Ship aroused interest at home and resulted in the return of such converts as missionaries to their native country.

In 1846, Ole Peter Petersen, a Norwegian sailor, was converted on board the Bethel Ship. His letters to his friends and fiancé, telling of the great change wrought in him, were passed around among relatives and friends until they were worn out by usage, and they stirred the first interest in Methodism. Petersen returned in 1849 for a visit of one month, but as he told his family and neighbors about Methodism their response and their insistent demands led him to remain for thirteen months, holding informal religious meetings.

Upon the return of Petersen to America in 1850, requests came from Norway to the Missionary Society of the Methodist Episcopal Church for a preacher, and in 1853 the Missionary Society appointed Petersen as the first Methodist missionary to Norway. He found the Norwegian people so eager to hear his message that it became difficult to secure halls large enough to accommodate the large audiences that sought to attend his evangelistic services.

Methodism expanded so rapidly in Norway that in 1856 Christian Willerup was sent as superintendent. In September, 1856, the first Methodist society was organized at Sarpsborg, and the next year the congregation erected the first Methodist church edifice in Norway. Soon there were Methodist societies in most of the towns and cities of Norway, and the Norway Annual Conference was organized in 1876.

DENMARK

In 1858 Christian Willerup was released from his position as superintendent in Norway in order to serve as a Methodist evangelist in all the Scandinavian countries. Being a Dane by birth, although converted in America, Willerup went in 1858 to his native country and began to preach in Copenhagen. He organized the first Methodist society in Denmark in January, 1859.

Willerup found, however, that a convert of the Bethel Ship, Boie Smith, a layman, had preceded him to Denmark. Because of his health, Smith had returned from America to Denmark and had supported himself by the sale of religious literature and had been appointed as a colporteur by the Missionary Society of the Methodist Episcopal Church.

Willerup and Smith preached in rented halls because the Danish laws forbade outdoor preaching. These halls proved too small, however, and in January, 1866, the first Methodist church in Denmark, St. Paul's Church at Copenhagen, with a seating capacity of one thousand, was dedicated. The Denmark Mission Conference was organized in 1900, and it became the Denmark Annual Conference in 1911.

FINLAND

Finland also was influenced by the Bethel Ship. Two Swedish-speaking Finnlanders, Gustaf and William Bernlund, who were converted on the Bethel Ship, returned to Finland in 1866 and began to preach in the Swedish language. Local preachers from Sweden volunteered their services, and by 1885 Methodism had made such progress among the Swedish-speaking people in Finland that the work in Finland was made a district of the Sweden Annual Conference.

In 1887 the Methodist message was extended to citizens of Finland who spoke the Finnish language. This work was advanced when, in 1891, the Finnish government granted the Methodists the right to organize societies and hold property on condition that persons who became Methodists would withdraw from the State Church of Finland.

In 1892 the Finland and St. Petersburg Mission was organized, including all Methodist activities in Finland and Russia. In 1911 Finnish Methodism became an annual conference separate from Russia. Then, because of the language difficulties, it was necessary in 1923 to divide Finnish Methodism into the Finland Annual Conference and the Finland-Swedish Mission Conference. Both groups have (1949) the status of provisional annual conferences.

SWITZERLAND

A noted Swiss preacher, John Fletcher, was one of the outstanding helpers of John Wesley in founding Methodism in England. Fletcher was born at Nyon, was converted in London in 1752, for many years was a Methodist preacher in England, and master of Kingswood School, the first Methodist educational institution. John Wesley even designated Fletcher as the logical person to be his successor as the leader of English Methodism.

Although the work of Fletcher was mainly in England, he returned to Switzerland in 1777 and for four years held meetings and organized Sunday Schools in French-speaking cantons. These did not, however, produce permanent Methodist congregations. It is interesting that the English Methodists in 1839 sent two preachers to Switzerland as a token of appreciation for the contributions made by Fletcher to English Methodism; they served in French-speaking cantons near the birthplace of Fletcher and in 1841 a Methodist society was formed at Lausanne.

Methodism in Switzerland today works mainly with the German-speaking Swiss and is the result of missionary activity on the part of German Methodist preachers. This was a natural development, since no passports or visas were required in the nineteenth century between Switzerland and Germany. The pietistic movement which had aided the progress of Methodism in Germany had a counterpart among the German-speaking citizens of Switzerland.

The first German Methodist preachers in Switzerland were Ernst Mann and Hermann zur Jakobsmuhlen. Mann preached his first sermon at Lausanne in February, 1856, while Jakobsmuhlen began his work at Zurich in October of the same year. The canton of Zurich, always known for its liberal religious and social policies, became the center from which Methodism spread to most of the cantons in northern and northwestern Switzerland.

The first converts in Switzerland were zealous in their endeavor to proclaim their new religion and a native ministry was soon available. Although some German preachers continued to work for many years in Switzerland, yet it was the native Swiss preachers and laymen who built Methodism in the country. In 1868 Swiss Methodism was included in the Germany and Switzerland Annual Conference, but in 1886 Switzerland became a separate annual conference.

AUSTRIA-HUNGARY

Because of the large number of Germans living in the Dual Monarchy of Austria-Hungary, German Methodists naturally became interested in carrying the Methodist message to people in the territory now comprising Austria, Hungary, and northern Yugoslavia. In 1870 Christian Dieterle was sent from Germany as the first Methodist preacher to Austria-Hungary. He labored for five years in Vienna, but because of the intolerant religious policy of Austria he was prohibited from holding public religious services.

Austrian Methodism was fortunate in having the support of the Baroness of Langenau, who, while traveling with her husband, an Austrian ambassador, had learned of Methodism. Upon returning to Vienna she affiliated with the persecuted Methodists and opened her home for a Sunday School. She supported the Methodist deaconess work in Austria and in 1881 purchased property for the use of the Methodists. Despite this assistance, Methodism made slow progress in Austria, and in 1890 there were fewer than forty members.

While Methodism was facing persecution in Austria, a Macedonian call came to the pastor in Vienna, Robert Möller, to come to Vrbas, Hungary, and preach to German-speaking people who had experienced a religious awakening. A teacher in Vrbas, Henrik Schmidt, had subscribed for the *Christliche Apologete,* the German Methodist periodical in America, and thereby had learned of Methodism. He formed a reading circle, and each week he read portions of the periodical to his friends and neighbors. From the paper Schmidt discovered that there was a Methodist preacher at Herisau, Switzerland. He wrote to the pastor, Johannes Haerle, who sent several other Methodist publications and the name and address of the Methodist preacher in Vienna. In this manner Robert Moller received the invitation to Vrbas. He accepted it, and began to preach in Vrbas and other parts of what was then southern Hungary, but which is now northern Yugoslavia.

In 1900 F. H. Otto Melle, then pastor of the Methodist church in Dresden, Germany, was appointed to Hungary. Under his leadership Methodism was founded in southern Hungary among both the German and Hungarian-speaking people. In 1905 Melle began work at Budapest among the Germans, and two years later Janos Tessenyi started Methodist services in the Hungarian language at Budapest. In 1907 Melle was appointed superintendent of all Methodist work in Austria-Hungary, which became in 1911 the Mission Conference of Austria-Hungary.

RUSSIA

Methodism entered Russia through the zeal of German and Finnish imigrants. After the partition of Poland in 1795, Germany and Russia had a common boundary, and many Germans worked in Russian factories and formed small German groups there. From one of these groups a young man, Heinrich Ramke, migrated to America, where he became a Methodist. With the zeal of a missionary he returned to Russia, and at Kowno in 1893 he organized a Methodist class and Sunday School. The German Methodists, being petitioned for a preacher, sent assistance and the work soon spread to Wilno, Wirballen and other cities. The first Methodist church edifice in Russia was dedicated at Wirballen on February 7, 1909.

Methodism also entered Russia from Finland. In 1889 B. A. Carlson, district superintendent in Finland, began to hold evangelistic meetings in St. Petersburg. In 1892 the congregations in Finland and Russia were incorporated into the Finland and St. Petersburg Mission. Services were held in St. Petersburg in Russian, Finnish and Swedish.

In 1907 George A. Simons, son of a German Methodist preacher in America, was appointed superintendent of the Finland and St. Petersburg Mission, with headquarters in St. Petersburg, and much progress was made under his leadership. In 1908 a Deaconess Home was organized at St. Petersburg under the supervision of Deaconess Anna Eklund. At one time there was a Methodist church in Siberia. The Bolshevist Revolution of 1917 prevented further growth of Methodism in Russia.

BULGARIA

Methodism began in Bulgaria in 1857, when that country was still under Turkish rule and a needy missionary field. Bishop William Burt has stated that the Bulgarian people "lay helpless between their twin masters, the Turkish governors and Greek ecclesiastics. The Greek clergy completed by their tyranny what the Turks began."

The Congregational Church had established missionary activity in southern Bulgaria and invited the Methodist Episcopal Church to enter the northern section. The invitation was accepted, and the first Methodist missionaries, Wesley Prettyman and Albert L. Long, reached Bulgaria in 1857. In 1892 the Bulgarian Mission Conference was organized.

Political unrest and war between Turkey and Bulgaria made missionary work very difficult. There was religious persecution, first under the Turks and then by Bulgarians after Bulgaria achieved independence. Few mission fields of Methodism have faced so many internal problems and lack of adequate support. Bishop William Burt declared in 1907: "Our policy has been vacillatory and critical. We have surrounded ourselves with restrictions and allowed others to dictate where we should go and what we should do. We have not so dealt with any other mission of the church." Bishop John L. Nuelsen once asserted: "Truly Methodism in no land in Europe found so hard and difficult a mission field as Bulgaria."

ITALY

Protestantism has been persecuted in Italy since Peter Waldo, a pre-reformer of the twelfth century, won converts in northern Italy. These pioneer Italian Protestants, the Waldensians, have had a noble history and tradition. Although they were native Italians, they were persecuted for centuries and were restricted to the Alpine valleys of northern Italy adjacent to France. Prior to 1870 no Waldensian or any other Protestant, except foreign diplomats, could hold public worship services in Rome, which was ruled by the pope in both religious and political affairs.

In view of the weakness of Italian Protestantism and the intolerant policy of Roman Catholicism, Italy was considered by Protestants of other countries as a field for evangelical effort. In 1859 an Italian monk, Bartolomeo Gualtieri, was converted and formed a Methodist congregation in Florence. He appealed to the Wesleyan Missionary Society in London for helpers, and in 1861 Richard Green and Henry Piggott were sent as the first missionaries of the English Methodists to Italy. They organized the Wesleyan Methodist Church. Because of sickness Green returned to England in 1863, but Piggott gave forty years of his life to Italian Methodism.

The unification of Italy in 1870, and the loss by the pope of political control, made possible the missionary activity of the Methodist Episcopal Church in Italy. In 1871 Leroy M. Vernon was sent by the Missionary Society to begin a Methodist mission. He mastered the Italian language and held the first service at Modena on June 16, 1873. With the help of native assistants Vernon extended the work, and in 1875 he was able to dedicate a Methodist church in Rome. In 1881 the Italy Annual Conference was organized. In 1886, William Burt, a member of the New York East Conference, was transferred to Italy, and from that date until his election to the episcopacy in 1904 he gave dynamic leadership to Italian Methodism. Italy became one of the most popular fields for missionary activity on the part of both the English and American Methodists.

FRANCE

Methodism first entered France from England; in fact, "France" was an appointment of the British Methodist Conference as early as 1791. The French Revolution and the Napoleonic period which followed made impossible the continuing of the work in France. There began, however, a Methodist movement among seventy thousand French prisoners of war in England during this period. In 1818 Charles Cook went from England as a Methodist missionary to France, and for forty years he was the leader of French Methodism. In 1852 the French Wesleyan Conference was organized.

The Methodist Episcopal Church had often been invited to send missionaries to France, but it was not until the separation of church and state in France in 1905 that the invitation was accepted. In May, 1907, under the leadership of Bishop William Burt, Methodist congregations were organized at Chambery, Grenoble, Lyons Avignon, and Marseilles, cities which had been neglected by other Protestant groups. The reason for this action was thus stated by Bishop Burt: "The papacy, oppressive, grasping and anti-democratic, has almost strangled the religious life of the nation, while Protestantism, often weak, selfishly narrow and rationalistic, has failed to measure up to its opportunity to lead the people back to their original simple faith." Another observer has stated that the religious struggle in France at the beginning of the twentieth century was not with a distorted conception of God, but with a refusal to worship God at all. It was estimated that in 1907 only one-fourth of the French people were practicing Christians. The French Mission of the Methodist Episcopal Church was officially organized in 1908.

SPAIN

Francisco Albricias was the founder of Episcopal Methodism in Spain, although prior to his work there had been British Methodist missionaries in the country. Albricias was born in 1856 at Barcelona of Roman Catholic parents. He was converted to Protestantism through a British Methodist teacher, and then secured his education in Switzerland. Upon returning to Spain he realized the great need of education for the Spanish youth, and in 1897 he began in a tent school for the children of Alicante. Unable by law to use the term Protestant in connection with his school, he chose the name, Model School (Escuela Modelo).

The Model School became recognized as one of the best schools in Spain, with an enrollment in 1920 of nine hundred students. Albricias also conducted religious services in his school and home; a Sunday School which began with only a few children later became the largest Protestant Sunday School in Spain.

The success of the Model School convinced Albricias that no single individual or family could provide sufficient resources or administration, and in 1919 he therefore offered his school to the Methodist Episcopal Church. Because of the great service being rendered by the school to evangelical Christianity in Spain, the offer was accepted. A second school, the Evangelical School at Seville, was also adopted by the Methodists. The congregation which had been founded at Alicante by Albricias became a Methodist church. The Spain Methodist Mission was organized in 1920. In that year Bishop John L. Nuelsen declared: "To the educational we hope soon to add the evangelical approach and build a vigorous type of evangelical Christianity into the life of the nation."

MADEIRA ISLANDS

Since 1876 there had been on the Madeira Islands an independent Protestant Mission, sponsored by William G. Smart and his father.

In answer to the appeal of this family, the Methodist Episcopal Church assumed supervision of the work, and in 1925 the scattered congregations were organized into the Madeira Methodist Mission.

BELGIUM, CZECHOSLOVAKIA, POLAND

The Methodist Episcopal Church, South, established Methodism in these three countries in connection with its relief program in Europe after World War I. Before the war ended Southern Methodists included in their Missionary Centenary budget a large appropriation for material and spiritual assistance to the victims of the war. Consultation with the Northern Methodist leaders resulted in the agreement that Belgium, Czechoslovakia and Poland should

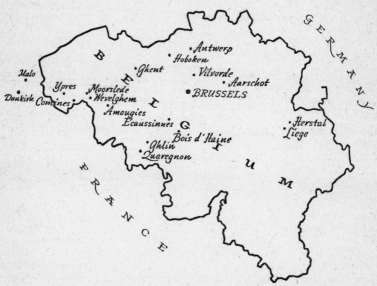

Belgium, showing principal centers of Methodist work

be the fields for this special service by the Methodist Episcopal Church, South.

A large relief program, which saved the lives of thousands of people, was promoted in Belgium, Czechoslovakia and Poland. Methodist relief centers providing soup kitchens, workshops, orphanages and other types of assistance were organized in many cities of these three war-devastated countries.

The relief program lasted for only a few years after the close of the war, but in that short time a demand had arisen for the continuation of Methodism as a spiritual force in these nations. Concerning this, Bishop John L. Nuelsen has written: "The impelling motive was the desire to help in the work of reconstruction after the havoc wrought by the war, the crying physical poverty, the moral needs, the religious destitution. The relief work was begun not with interest to proselyte but to render help in building up what had been destroyed by war. This humanitarian work had its source in an intense evangelistic urge and was accompanied by continuous evangelism."

BELGIUM

Concerning the origin of Methodism in Belgium, Dr. W. G. Thonger, superintendent of the Belgian Methodist Mission, has written as follows: "Those of us who at that time were called upon to carry out this post-war relief were soon quite conscious of the fact that material and physical ruins can be repaired more easily and quickly than the moral and spiritual devastation of war. So, quite logically and inevitably, this temporary post-war relief program carried out by a missionary church became an evangelistic missionary effort." The weakness of Belgian Protestantism and the breaking away of many Belgians from the Roman Catholic Church were other reasons for the evangelistic effort of Methodism. In August, 1922, the Belgian Methodist Mission was organized.

In regard to the evangelistic program of early Belgian Methodism Dr. Thonger has stated: "Many interesting details could be given about the methods used to bring the Gospel to the Belgian people with Gospel-tents, intensive open-air work, door to door

Bible colportage and religious services in rented ballrooms, drinking saloons and any other premises which could be secured. Much time was given to the preparation and circulation of suitable literature. For example, our evangelistic and Bible colporteurs found that in the industrial sections, especially in the mining districts, the working classes would not accept Gospels or New Testaments because they looked like 'Mass-Books' or 'Priest-Books,' so the New Testament was printed in newspaper form, both in French and Flemish, and these papers sold so rapidly that several editions were necessary."

CZECHOSLOVAKIA

There were many reasons for the interest of Southern Methodism in 1918 in the new republic of Czechoslovakia. The tragic history of that country made a special appeal. It was a Bohemian, John Huss, who had been burned at the stake at the Council of Constance in 1415 by the Roman Catholic Church. The martyrdom of Huss caused the Bohemian people to reject allegiance to the papacy, and by the end of the sixteenth century Bohemia and Moravia had become ninety per cent Protestant.

The coming of the Hapsburg dynasty to the throne of Bohemia brought both autocracy and intolerance. The Hapsburg rulers began a fanatical attack upon Protestantism. During the rule of Ferdinand II (1619-1637) Protestantism in Bohemia and Moravia was ruthlessly crushed by force. After 1620 Protestant worship was forbidden and even the ownership of a Bible or a Protestant hymnal was a crime. For one hundred and sixty-one years, until 1781, Protestants were not tolerated in the land of John Huss.

It was, however, from the descendants of these Bohemian and Moravian Protestants that John Wesley came into contact with vital religion. He met exiled Moravian leaders on his trip to Georgia in 1735, and Peter Bohler, a Moravian preacher, led Wesley to his Aldersgate experience in London on May 24, 1738. Thus early Methodism was closely connected with the Moravians both in England and America.

The relief program of Southern Methodism coincided with a

great evangelistic movement in Czechoslovakia. Because the Haps-
burgs had forced Roman Catholicism in religion and autocracy
in government upon the Czechoslovak people, it was felt by many
in 1918 that release from the autocratic Hapsburg regime should
involve freedom from the papacy. In a great "Free from Rome"
movement, two million Czechs left the Roman Catholic Church
between 1918 and 1926. Such a movement offered a great opportunity for Methodist evangelism.

By an interesting providence there were at that moment several
preachers in the American Church who were able to preach in the
Czech language. They were Czechs who had migrated to Texas,
where they had become Methodist preachers and American citizens.
Two of these, Joseph Dobes and J. P. Bartak, returned as missionaries to Czechoslovakia, and under their leadership great
evangelistic meetings were held in tents and in the largest halls
available in Czechoslovakia. Thousands were converted, and by
August, 1922, the Czechoslovak Methodist Mission was organized.

POLAND

The Methodist Episcopal Church, South, entered Poland as
a relief agency after World War I because the conditions in the
new republic in 1918 were appalling. Millions of men, women and
children were destitute and many were starving. In order to help
these people the Southern Methodists inaugurated a movement
to secure food, clothing and other relief supplies. In a spectacular
campaign, more than one million garments and other articles valued
at $2,000,000 were collected and a special ship was chartered to
transport the materials to Poland. In various centers of the country
the Methodist relief stations were established; in Warsaw alone
there were ten soup kitchens feeding three thousand people daily.
Speedy and extensive service enabled the Methodists to save the
lives of thousands of Polish people.

When the immediate need for physical relief had passed, Methodism found itself established in various cities of Poland, and many
persons who had been recipients of its temporal ministry were

eager for its spiritual message. Polish immigrants who had been converted in America asked for the organization of Methodist churches in the new Poland. The new Polish boundaries also included some former German Methodist congregations. It was found that in eastern Poland, among the White Russians, there were many villages with little or no religious instruction. When hundreds of Polish people began to apply for Methodist membership, the Poland-Danzig Mission of the Methodist Episcopal Church, South, was organized in August, 1922.

Conclusion

From the above brief accounts it will be seen that Methodism entered Europe through four methods.

1. European immigrants converted abroad were primarily responsible for founding the church in Germany, Sweden, Denmark, Norway and Finland. As Bishop John L. Nuelsen has stated: "Historically speaking, European Methodism is a reflex of European immigration to America, and, in a less degree, to England."

2. The European Methodists have always been missionary in theory and practice. From Germany, Methodism was carried to Switzerland, Russia, Austria, Hungary and Yugoslavia. In like manner the Finnish Methodists exerted missionary efforts in Russia.

3. There have always been countries in Europe which, because of the weakness of native Protestantism, have been considered as special fields of Protestant missionary activity. It was thus that Methodism entered Bulgaria, Italy, Spain, the Madeira Islands and France.

4. Methodism in Belgium, Czechoslovakia and Poland is the result of Southern Methodist relief activity after World War I. It was felt that real reconstruction in these countries involved a spiritual ministry as well as material assistance.

It has occasionally been stated that European Methodism represents an attempt on the part of American Methodists to enlarge the sphere of their influence by establishing missions in Europe and by proselyting Europeans. To this unfair statement

Bishop John L. Nuelsen gave the following appropriate answer in 1924: "Let it be stated most emphatically that we are not in Europe merely to build up our own ecclesiastical organization at the expense of other evangelistic bodies. We are not wasting our time or our money in an attempt to make Methodists out of Lutherans or even of Catholics. Small business this would be . . . unworthy of a large body of Christians in these harrowing times. We are here by Divine Providence to assist other followers of Christ in their impossible task, to bear our share of the common burden, and to make our contribution to the religious, moral, social and economic life of Continental Europe."

DISCUSSION SUGGESTIONS

1. Stress the fact, and the significance of the fact, that in many European countries Methodism arose as the result of the letters, testimony and preaching of immigrants from those countries who were converted in America. Point out that a home mission enterprise had world-wide repercussions.

2. Emphasize the romantic story of the Bethel Ship and its influence in all the Scandinavian countries. Write to the Editorial Department, 150 Fifth Ave., New York 11, N. Y., for free copies of a folder entitled "Bethelship" for use in the class.

3. Trace the spread of Methodism to Austria, Hungary, and elsewhere as the result of the preaching of Methodists from Germany.

4. What were the four methods by which Methodism reached continental Europe?

Scandinavia

CHAPTER II

THE METHODIST MESSAGE AND PROGRAM

BETWEEN 1830 and 1922 Methodist societies were organized in most of the European nations, and into these countries was carried the traditional Methodist message and program.

The European Methodists, like their brethren elsewhere, did not stress a peculiar type of theology. Their doctrines were those of John Wesley, "simply the common fundamental principles of Christianity." They emphasized something greater and more noble than theology, namely, the living of a good life. Applicants for membership were asked the two historic Wesleyan questions: "Is thy heart right?" "Dost thou love and serve God?"

Instead of theology, they emphasized Christian experience. They told and retold the Aldersgate religious experience of John Wesley, and they preached the gospel of a "warmed heart." Under their preaching such historic doctrines as justification by faith, the witness of the Spirit, the universality of the atonement, and the possibility of Christian perfection had a new meaning because of the vitality that came from the experiences of the messengers. To many people the Methodist message of full, free and present salvation, with an assurance of the forgiveness of sin, was almost a revelation. Dr. Adolf Keller, the Swiss church historian, says that in view of the deplorable state of spiritual life among the European churches in the nineteenth century the message of Methodism was as new and as fresh as when preached by John Wesley.

European Methodists were concerned with giving the historic Christian doctrines a vital power in the lives of individuals, and they injected the truths into the hearts and emotions of people. In brief, Methodism was offered to Europe not as a philosophy or a theology, but as a religious experience causing men and women to exemplify the Christian ideals in contact with their neighbors.

This of course, was a common idea among Methodists everywhere, but on the continent it was new and startling.

To the superficial European observer this lack of emphasis on theology could be considered as heretical. John Wesley declared that "the distinguishing marks of a Methodist are not his opinions of any sort," and that "We do not lay the main stress of our religion on opinions, right or wrong; neither do we begin, nor willingly join in any dispute concerning them." Wesley refused to become excited about non-essential matters, or waste time arguing over petty theological issues.

It should always be remembered, however, that this was a reversal of the continental process. When Methodism entered Europe the State Churches were stressing creeds and demanding verbal allegiance to doctrines which were often not understood by the average person and meant little in daily living. Despite its emphasis on creeds and dogmas, however, European Protestantism in many places in the nineteenth century had become infected with rationalism.

European Methodism has been richly rewarded for its sane theology. There have been no schisms over doctrinal issues. By stressing Christian experience and the witness of the Spirit in the life of an individual, Methodism offered a haven of refuge to many devout Christians who were disturbed by the rationalism that hampered many sections of European Protestantism at that time.

EVANGELISM

The Methodists of Europe have never considered that their religion was a private possession, but rather that it must be shared with other people. Evangelism has therefore been an outstanding characteristic. Even before church edifices could be erected, the Methodists held evangelistic meetings in halls, private homes, tents and on the streets and public squares. One hundred years ago such an evangelistic approach was a novelty in Europe, and Methodist evangelism was attacked and criticized in some countries as degrading religion. Many men and women, however, who were estranged from the State Churches were inspired by the Methodist evangelists who proclaimed the simple but effective Wesleyan message.

Another characteristic of European Methodism was the informality of the worship services. Methodist sermons, characterized by evangelistic fervor, were in contrast with the essays of some State Church pastors. Not only did the Methodist preachers offer extemporaneous prayers, but many laymen in the congregations did likewise. The hymns of Charles Wesley were taken to the continent, and the singing of the great Wesleyan hymns made the European Methodists happy people, not only in their public and private worship, but also in their daily activities.

MORAL CONDUCT

Converts were required to exemplify their religion by high moral and ethical conduct. Other-worldliness and self-denial characterized the pioneer European Methodists. It was believed that conversion meant both an inward and an outward change; that a loyal Methodist would have no desire for worldly things. To enable his first followers in England to keep themselves "unspotted from the world," John Wesley had in 1743 published the "General Rules," a series of practical daily regulations. Although general in nature, these rules pointed out the things which were to be avoided by those who desired "to flee from the wrath to come, and to be saved from their sins," and they cautioned the Methodists against "taking such diversions as cannot be used in the name of the Lord Jesus."

In endeavoring to follow these regulations the European Methodists became known for their high code of personal morality. They held that there were few amusements that could be used in the name of the Saviour. Dancing was banned. A loyal Methodist did not attend theaters and carnivals. Card playing was condemned. It was not considered a Christian characteristic to wear fashionable clothes or use jewelry. Members were dropped from the societies for breaches of discipline. It is no surprise that pleasure-loving European people regarded the Methodists as pietists.

European Methodists became recognized as opponents of both public and private vice. For example, they were the pioneers in the fight in Europe against the use of intoxicating liquors. They carried to the front the banner of total abstinence in the face of ridicule and scorn. It has been stated that the attack in European countries upon alcohol began with the appearance of Methodist preachers. Although George Scott was forced to leave Sweden in 1842, yet during his stay there he organized the first total abstinence society in Sweden. By their attacks upon alcoholic beverages the Methodists soon won the enmity of those who made financial profit from the liquor traffic, because a convert to Methodism meant a customer lost for the taverns and cafés. In like manner European Methodists were the foes of gambling, Sabbath desecration, swearing, dueling and similar social evils.

A SOCIAL PROGRAM

The European Methodists, however, had more than a negative policy concerning social evils, for they also emulated the constructive social program of Methodism started by John Wesley: "If a man would serve God whom he has not seen, he must serve man whom he has seen." Wesley had asserted that true religion, in addition to spiritual aid, also consisted in giving food to the hungry, in clothing the naked, in visiting the sick, and in rendering social and economic assistance to all types of needy people. The European Methodists endeavored to put into practice that social doctrine.

John Wesley in 1748 established a home for orphans in connection with the Foundry, the first Methodist chapel in London. In like manner the European Methodists founded orphanages. There are (1949) thirty-two Methodist orphanages in Europe, some of which have been in existence for many years. Besides permanent homes for orphans, the Methodists also organized day nurseries where children are cared for while their mothers work in factories and offices. They have also founded and supported homes for aged people. There are twenty-four such Methodist homes in Europe, located in Germany, Sweden, Denmark, Finland, Norway, Switzerland, Yugoslavia, Hungary, Poland, Czechoslovakia and Austria.

In addition to providing orphanages and homes for the aged, the European Methodists, especially in the Scandinavian countries, endeavored to follow the pattern set by John Wesley at the Foundry by making local churches the relief centers for needy people. The best example of this type of service is the Central Mission in Copenhagen, Denmark, which was founded in 1910 by Anton Bast in connection with the Jerusalem Methodist Church there. A large social program was developed which included homes for orphans, a hostel for young people, a soup kitchen, nursery for infants, shelter for unemployed men, and relief employment for dependent people. By 1928 the annual budget of the Central Mission was in excess of $100,000, most of which was contributed by non-Methodists. The success of the Central Mission led to the founding of similar institutions in other Scandinavian countries.

THE DEACONESS MOVEMENT

The traditional Methodist social program was extended when in 1874 the German and Swiss Methodists founded the Methodist deaconess movement, which has been adopted in America and elsewhere. It began as a nursing ministry and Methodist girls desiring to render special social service under religious auspices received training as nurses and became members of a Methodist Deaconess Society. Wearing a special deaconess uniform, they served in Methodist hospitals, in state hospitals, and as private nurses in homes. Although all deaconesses are required to have training as nurses, some are appointed as leaders in student hostels and assistants in local churches.

The Methodist deaconesses have been aptly described as sisters of mercy ministering not only to physical needs, but also rendering spiritual assistance. They have carried the Gospel directly and indirectly to places in Europe where ordained clergymen often were not permitted. They have especially rendered a spiritual service among the working classes.

The Methodist deaconess movement was at first confined to Germany and Switzerland, but it was later extended to the Scandinavian countries, Austria, Russia, Yugoslavia and Hungary. It was also adopted by American Methodism. There are nearly two thousand deaconesses in European Methodism (1949).

In connection with the deaconess program Methodist hospitals, sanatoriums and convalescent homes were founded in various parts of Europe. There are thirty-six of these institutions, in which more than two hundred thousand patients receive treatment annually.

The Missionary Urge

The European Methodists have always been interested in home and foreign missions. Hardly had Methodism been established in countries of Europe before annual collections were made for foreign missions. In 1875 the collections in Swedish Methodism for missionary enterprises were four times larger than the combined salaries of all Swedish Methodist preachers, and this record has probably never been equalled in any other conference anywhere.

European Methodism has furnished many foreign missionaries. From Germany and Switzerland missionaries went to Austria, Hungary and Yugoslavia. By 1907 the Swedish Methodists were able to support two of their group in Portuguese East Africa. In 1914 German Methodist missionaries were working in German West Africa and New Guinea. The first Swiss Methodist missionary, Miss Hedwig Graf, went to West Africa. This interest in foreign missions led to the formation of independent Methodist Missionary Societies in the Scandinavian countries, Germany and Switzerland, but these remained as auxiliary agencies of the Board of Missions of American Methodism.

CHRISTIAN EDUCATION

The Wesleyan interest in Christian education became a characteristic of continental Methodism. This was especially evident in the founding of Sunday Schools, youth organizations and educational institutions.

The early European Methodists were the most active promoters of the Sunday School movement. At a time when the State Churches did not have Sunday Schools, the Methodists organized them in many places, and some of them had as many as one thousand pupils. It became necessary for the State Churches to adopt the Sunday School because of the popularity of the Methodist Sunday Schools among the children of State Church parishes.

The Epworth League became very popular. By 1924 the Epworth Leagues of Denmark were paying the salary of one of their former members then serving in the Belgian Congo. After a visit to Norway in 1928, Bishop Edgar Blake declared that the Methodist Young People's Societies were equal to the best youth groups in American Methodism. On the eve of World War II there were nearly eighty thousand young people enrolled in Methodist youth societies.

The Methodists early realized the need of schools for the children of the poor. The educational systems of some European nations did not provide education for the poor, and many of the state schools were rationalistic. Among the outstanding schools sponsored or supported by European Methodists have been the American School at Lovetch, Bulgaria; Crandon International Institute, Rome, Italy; Collegio Internazionale at Monte Mario, Rome, Italy; Industrial School at Venice, Italy; School for Girls at Novi Sad, Yugoslavia; English Language School, Warsaw, Poland; Methodist School, Klarysew, Poland; Les Marronniers, Brussels, Belgium; Model School, Alicante, Spain; Evangelical School, Seville, Spain; Girls' Schools, Grenoble, France. Although most of these schools are no longer in existence, yet their founding showed that the European Methodists accepted the view of John Wesley that "the Methodists may be poor but there is no reason they should be ignorant."

European Methodism has also believed in a trained ministry, and from its beginning undertook to organize theological seminaries. The first Methodist theological seminary in Europe was founded at Bremen, Germany, in 1858; it was later moved to Frankfurt-am-Main and is owned jointly by the German and Swiss Methodists. In 1874 a theological seminary for Swedish Methodism was founded at Orebo, while Danish Methodists began in the same year a similar school in Copenhagen. A Norwegian Methodist seminary was founded in 1888 at Christiana, while the Finnish Methodists organized their school at Helsingfors in 1897. In 1924 the Union Scandinavian School of Theology at Gothenburg, Sweden, was established to provide further graduate study. Other Methodist theological schools were founded at Florence, Italy, in 1888; Prague, Czechoslovakia, in 1922; Brussels, Belgium, in 1922; Warsaw, Poland, in 1927.

RELIGIOUS LITERATURE

One of the first actions taken by John Wesley in the Methodist revival was to spread religious information by the printed page. He opened at the Foundry a book room for the sale of literature and by his own pen he began to furnish the poor people with inexpensive religious and secular books and tracts. In 1778 he began the publication of *The Arminian Magazine,* the first Methodist periodical in the world.

The European Methodists followed this program of John Wesley and for the same reasons. They found very little religious literature for the masses available in Roman Catholic and State Church circles. In Protestant countries religious literature too often consisted of scholarly doctrinal essays which did not have a large circulation among the people. To remedy this the European Methodists began the publication and distribution of their own literature and much use was made of colporteurs.

On May 21, 1850, less than six months after he had reached Germany, L. S. Jacoby issued the first copy of *Der Evangelist.*

Other famous European Methodist periodicals are *Svenska Sandebudet* (1868) of Sweden; *Kristelig Tidende* (1872) of Norway; *Kristelig Talsman* (1873) of Denmark; *Nya Budbararen* (1886) and *Rauhan Sanoma* (1894) of Finland; *Schweizer Evangelist* (1893) of Switzerland; *l'Evangelista* (1889) of Italy; *Oesterreichischer Evangelist* (1911) of Austria; *Bekeharang* (1910) of Hungary; *Krestansky Buditel* (1922) of Czechoslovakia; *Pielgrzym Polski* (1922) of Poland; *La Bonne Nouvelle* (1922) and *Le Messager Méthodiste* (1948) of Belgium.

This interest in literature led to the founding of Methodist publishing houses. In 1856 a Methodist Publishing House was founded at Bremen, Germany. Since then publishing houses have been founded by Methodists in other countries as follows: Sweden (1873), Finland (1886), Norway (1867), Switzerland (1892), Italy (1897), Denmark (1900). In Austria, Belgium, Yugoslavia, Poland and Czechoslovakia, the Methodists maintain bookstores for the sale of religious literature.

In some countries, especially those with Roman Catholic and Orthodox backgrounds, the Methodists printed and furnished Bibles to the people. In Bulgaria a Methodist missionary, Dr. Albert L. Long, in cooperation with Dr. Rigg of the Congregational Church in 1870 translated the Bible into the Bulgarian language, and the distribution of the Bible became a recognized Protestant contribution to Bulgaria. Finally, in 1925, the Orthodox Church also translated and published the Bible in the Bulgarian language. One of their leaders stated that the Orthodox Church was compelled to do this because many Bulgarian people believed that the distribution of the Scriptures was a monopoly of Protestantism.

A Free Church

The most striking feature of Methodism on the continent of Europe, however, was its status as a "Free Church," meaning a church free from state control or support and based upon the principle of voluntary membership and voluntary financial support. This was a radical innovation in the European countries, where for centuries the people had been taught to think of a church, Protestant, Roman Catholic or Orthodox, as related to the state and receiving its finances from taxes levied by the government.

Methodism has always held that the union of the church with the state is a dangerous absurdity, and the Free Church principle has been and is now one of its greatest contributions to European Protestantism. As Dr. Paul F. Douglass says: "The force of Methodism in keeping attention centered upon Christian freedom as a spontaneous fellowship of believers, unconcerned with the power of the state, must remain as one of its chief contributions to the Old World."

Map of Poland, showing centers of Methodist Work

The Methodists entered European countries which were accustomed to state-bound and state-supported churches. Bishop John L. Nuelsen states that Methodism offered instead of "state-churches a self-supporting Free Church, the membership of which is not compulsory, not regulated by state law, but voluntary, constrained by the love of Jesus Christ, under the compulsion of experiential, evangelistic and social passion." Methodism during the past century has actually demonstrated to Europe that a church can live by the voluntary support of its members and that there is no necessity to rely upon the political state for support. Dr. Adolf Keller, in referring to Methodism and other Free Churches in Europe, has said: "They were not separated by the state, but separated themselves much earlier, of their own free will, in order to keep the Church pure from the worldly influences and to maintain the principle of evangelical liberty, not only in their spiritual life, but in constitution and administration as well."

THE CLASS MEETING

The traditional features of Methodist polity, such as class meetings, conferences, lay activities, itinerant ministry and episcopacy, have always characterized European Methodism. Many of these were in contrast to the polity of the Protestant State Churches.

All Methodists were expected to be members of a small class that met each week. A layman served as class leader and made a public examination of the spiritual progress of each member, praising, admonishing or exhorting as the case demanded. The meetings began and ended with periods of prayer.

The class meeting was to a great extent responsible for the intimate fellowship which characterized European Methodism. A Christian brotherhood was developed among the members, who learned to know each other. Each new convert found himself one of a group bound together by common spiritual aspirations and from the class he received inspiration. The class meeting became a counteracting influence against the evils of daily life. The individual was not lost sight of in the expanding Methodist organization.

The European Methodists also made use of laymen in evangelistic and social programs. The number of laymen giving voluntary service has always exceeded by far the number of ordained preachers. There are (1949) one thousand ordained preachers in European Methodism, but there are two thousand laymen serving as local preachers. In addition there are approximately five thousand other lay helpers, such as exhorters, class leaders and Sunday School teachers.

The use of laymen by Methodism was a novelty in nineteenth century Europe, for in the State Churches there was a wide gulf between ordained clergymen and priests and the members of the congregations. Many of the Methodist lay helpers later became ordained preachers. Coming from the masses, they spoke the language of the average person, and they brought an understanding of the conditions of the industrial workers and their messages attracted the laboring classes. Many of the strongest local churches are among the industrial workers of the large cities.

The Conferences

The annual conference, another feature of Methodist polity, was also characteristic of European Methodism. At these annual meetings the preachers gave reports of their work, plans were made for the ensuing year and the preachers were appointed to the pastorates according to the prevalent usage among American Methodists. There are (1949) eleven annual conferences on the continent of Europe, with six provisional and five mission conferences.

With the growth of Methodism there came the normal desire of members for some form of autonomy. To make this possible, the General Conference of the Methodist Episcopal Church adopted the plan of the Central Conferences to provide for national autonomy for Methodists in countries outside of America, while permitting them to remain within the framework of world Methodism. In accordance with legislation enacted in 1924, a Northern European Central Conference, comprising the annual conferences and mission conferences of the Stockholm Area, was held at Oslo, Norway, in September, 1924. The Central European Conference for the Zurich Area was held at Freudenstadt, Germany, in October, 1925. Steps were taken at both of these conferences to adjust the Methodist program in conformity with special European conditions. The policy since 1924 has been to give additional powers to the Central Conferences, and in the near future all places of leadership in European Methodism will be held by Nationals.

EPISCOPACY

Episcopacy has also been a characteristic of European Methodism. Until 1900 episcopal supervision was provided by the annual visits of bishops who were also in charge of annual conferences in America. Upon the request, however, of the delegates from the European conferences, the General Conference of 1900 created the Zurich Area and John H. Vincent became the first resident bishop. He was succeeded in 1904 by William Burt, who served eight years as episcopal leader of European Methodism.

In 1912 John L. Nuelsen became bishop of the Zurich Area, and it is recognized that of all the bishops assigned to European Methodism, he rendered the most constructive service. Although an American citizen, Bishop Nuelsen was born at Zurich, Switzerland, where his father was serving as one of the pioneer Methodist preachers in Europe. He was educated in Switzerland, Germany and America, and could use fluently the languages of the people whom he served. He remained from 1912 to 1940 in Europe, giving the longest period of service of any bishop to European Methodism.

The contributions of Bishop Nuelsen were many. He was a scholar of international reputation and impressed European Protestants with his theological learning. Traveling back and forth almost annually between America and Europe, he became the bridge between American and continental theological views and practices and he brought an international viewpoint to European Methodism. He was deeply spiritual, but linked this with orderly procedure. He gave high tone to the educational program of his church.

The expansion of Methodism required additional episcopal

leaders. At the General Conference of 1920, Anton Bast, a Danish pastor, was elected bishop and assigned to the Scandinavian Area. He was succeeded by Bishop Raymond J. Wade, who served from 1928 to 1940. Under his wise leadership, Scandinavian Methodism was able to develop further, and the North Europe Central Conference in 1946 chose Theodor Arvidson as bishop.

The Paris Area, including France, Italy, Yugoslavia, Spain, Bulgaria and North Africa, was created by the General Conference of 1920, but was absorbed in 1932 into other episcopal areas. The bishops who served the Paris Area were Edgar Blake, 1920-1928, and William R. Shepherd, 1928-1931.

In 1936 the annual conferences in Germany became the Germany Central Conference and F. H. Otto Melle became the first German Methodist bishop. He was succeeded in 1946 by Bishop J. W. E. Sommer.

When the annual conferences of the Methodist Episcopal Church, South, were organized in 1922 in Poland, Czechoslovakia and Belgium, episcopal supervision was exercised by Bishop W. B. Beauchamp, the virtual founder of the work. His successor in 1926, Bishop U. V. W. Darlington, faced the hard problems incident to retrenchment during the financial depression. From 1934 to 1940 Bishop Arthur J. Moore served these annual conferences, his tenure being marked by a missionary passion and evangelistic fervor.

At the Uniting Conference of 1939 the Methodist annual conferences and mission conferences not included in the Stockholm Area and the Germany Central Conference were organized into the Central and Southern Europe Provisional Central Conference. Because of the outbreak of World War II, Bishop W. W. Peele and Bishop Arthur J. Moore, assigned in 1940 and 1942 respectively to this area, were unable to make episcopal visitations. In 1944 Bishop Paul N. Garber was assigned.

DISCUSSION SUGGESTIONS

1. Emphasize the features of early Methodism that were carried over into the Methodist churches on the continent.
2. What is meant by a "Free Church"?
3. What is the present organization of continental Methodism? Name the Central Conferences, Annual Conferences, Provisional Annual Conferences, etc.
4. What is the difference, administratively, between the Northern Europe and the Germany Central Conferences and the Geneva Area?

Chapter III

METHODISTS UNDER PERSECUTION

AFTER a study of the message and program of the European Methodists, it is difficult to understand why these peaceful people should have been persecuted, but the records show that they have been attacked in almost every nation of Europe. The basic reason for this is to be found in the union of church and state which has for centuries affected the religious and political life of the continent.

In the middle of the nineteenth century there were three large religious groups in Europe, namely, the Roman Catholic Church, the Orthodox Church, and the Protestant State Churches. It is to be regretted that religious toleration was not at that time a major characteristic of any of them.

The Roman Catholic Church

The Roman Catholic Church was dominant in Italy, Spain, Austria, Poland, Hungary, Belgium, France and Czechoslovakia. It also had many members in Germany and Switzerland. Although it was a minority church in these two countries, yet it had the status of a State Church.

The historic claim of the Roman Catholic Church is that Jesus Christ gave to Peter, one of the twelve apostles, the supreme control of the church on earth, this being based upon a unique interpretation of Matthew 16:13-19. According to this tradition Peter went to Rome, founded there the Roman Catholic Church, and passed on his power to a successor, later to be known as the pope. Competent historians have proved the falsity of this position, and have shown that the Roman Catholic Church and the papacy gained power through normal historical developments and not through any special divine plan.

47

With the growth of the Roman Catholic Church there developed the theory that salvation could be secured only through the sacramental system of that church, and that outside of the Roman Catholic Church there could be no salvation. Pope Gregory VII, who ruled from 1073 to 1085, asserted that the pope was entrusted by God with supreme oversight and control of all human society and that the pope was superior to secular rulers. The Middle Ages were marked with conflicts between the popes and the kings and emperors over this theory of papal supremacy.

Since the Roman Catholic Church held that it alone provided salvation, it logically followed it could not have fraternal relations with other religious groups, and that position is maintained today in every country of the world. A hostile policy was adopted toward heretics, and the threat of excommunication was held over any who dared to violate the traditional policy of the church. The papacy approved the use of the Inquisition to eradicate heresy, and thousands of Christians were put to death during the Middle Ages because they held independent religious views contrary to the teachings of the Roman Catholic Church.

When Methodism entered Europe in the nineteenth century, the Roman Catholic Church had lost much of its former power, but in many countries it still exercised a major influence in political affairs. It had never withdrawn its claim of being the only one true church and thereby having exclusive control of the salvation of all people. The Methodists were regarded as heretics and were subject to attack and persecution.

THE ORTHODOX CHURCH

The Orthodox Church in the nineteenth century was the major religious group in Russia, Bulgaria, Yugoslavia and Greece, and had members also in Poland, Hungary, Austria and Czechoslovakia. This church, known also as the Greek Orthodox Church or the Eastern Orthodox Church, had until 1054 been considered a part of the Roman Catholic Church, although the patriarch at Constantinople had always denied the papal claims and had consid-

ered himself equal with the pope at Rome. In 1054 the pope excom-
municated the Orthodox Christians as schismatics.

The Orthodox Church has been characterized by its stress upon
mysticism and ritualism. It has always been closely related to the
state and, like the Roman Catholic Church, has been subsidized
through state taxation. In Russia the Orthodox Church became one
of the recognized pillars of the Czarist regime, and it tended to
become oblivious to the sufferings of the masses. Having failed to
defend the liberties of the people and to champion justice for the
underprivileged classes, the Orthodox Church suffered much during
the Bolshevik revolution in Russia.

Since the Orthodox Church was the only State Church in certain European countries, it was able to secure legislation hostile to
other religious groups. As a result the Methodists were often
attacked in nations where the Orthodox Church was officially connected with the state. It refused to recognize Methodism as a
church, giving it instead the invidious designation of a "sect."

PROTESTANT STATE CHURCHES

It is to be regretted that the Protestant Reformation did not
include among its many virtues the separation of church and state.
It did not produce a Protestantism in Europe free from state control. The great Reformation leaders, Martin Luther, Huldreich
Zwingli and John Calvin, while proclaiming the freedom of the
church, permitted it to become entangled in a new way with state
affairs. Dr. Adolf Keller says: "At Luther's time, the Church,
although preaching the *sola fide,* had not the courage to build herself up on the Word of God and on trust in His guidance. She sought
shelter under the roof of the state. She borrowed from the state
the essential elements of her spiritual and administrative organization, and therefore, instead of being the witness of God among
men, became an annex or a department or a ward of the state."
Again Dr. Keller writes: "With the acceptance of the principle
cujus regio illius religio, especially in Germany, the Church was
entirely delivered into the hands of the state or the prince." The

Lutheran and Reformed movements developed into Protestant State Churches in Germany, Norway, Sweden, Denmark, Finland, Hungary and Switzerland. As late as 1918 the German emperor was *summus episcopus* of the Prussian State Church by virtue of his position as king of Prussia.

In the Protestant State Churches membership was not dependent upon formal declaration of faith but on birth, for any child born of Protestant parents was considered a member of the State Church of his locality. In other words, one was born into the church; his religious affiliation was not voluntary but was imposed by the state. There were several recognized Protestant State Churches. In Germany there were three: in Bavaria and Saxony the State Church was Lutheran; in Baden and the Rhineland it was Reformed; in Prussia, after a forced union of the Lutheran and Reformed groups under Frederick William III in 1817, the Union Church of Prussia became the State Church.

The State Churches were not supported by voluntary contributions but by taxes levied upon all citizens and by subsidies granted by the various legislative bodies. The pastors received their salaries from the state and were looked upon both as state officials and church leaders. The fact that the state furnished the financial support tended to make the church a department of the state and often even a tool of the state.

One result was that there arose a formalistic type of religion in many of the State Churches. One observer has described it as follows: "The life of the churches is usually dogmatic, slow, formal, liturgical, shy of idealism, far removed from that glorious freedom in life and joy in service which many have found in the Saviour." Preaching was usually theological in nature and often not understood by the average parishioner. Parishes often contained as many as twenty thousand members, making it impossible for the pastor and his assistants to have contact with the people. Although the State Churches claimed that religious facilities were provided for all people, such did not prove to be the case. There was usually a shortage of pastors, especially in the rural areas.

Although there were many devout leaders in the State Churches, there was in the nineteenth century very little emphasis on the evangelical phases of Christianity. The State Churches did not emphasize the work of the Sunday School and similar Protestant agencies. Home and foreign missionary work were not considered major functions of the church, but rather of societies with or without church connection. There was no place for special religious activity by the laymen, and social service work too often was turned over to secular and even non-religious groups. In many such churches there was a tendency toward rationalism, and this was accentuated by the fact that the state maintained the theological seminaries and appointed the teachers. Many of these teachers, losing contact with local church activities, created an atmosphere in the classroom that aided the growth of rationalism.

The basic theory of the Protestant State Church system was the ancient belief in the possibility of a Christian state. That had however, become a fiction, for the modern European states were not only not Christian but some were anti-Christian and even anti-religious. Nevertheless, the fiction was maintained. For example, persons participated in the election of pastors and voted on local ecclesiastical matters simply because they lived in parishes, even though they might be atheists or Communists.

A tragic aspect of the European Protestant State Churches was a lack of toleration for those individuals who desired to deviate from this ecclesiastical plan. The Reformation gave religious liberty primarily to the secular rulers, but the latter apparently were afraid to grant it to the masses. Legislation gave Protestant State Churches a monopoly on religious activities for all citizens except Jews, Roman Catholics and Orthodox members.

In order to understand better the problems faced by the pioneer Methodists in Europe brief accounts will be given of the discriminations practiced against them in each country, beginning with the nations in which the Protestant State Churches were dominant.

SWEDEN

After the Protestant Reformation the Lutheran Church became the State Church of Sweden. Only State Church clergymen could conduct public religious meetings for Swedish citizens. No foreign religious group using the Swedish language was permitted. The king of Sweden was required to be a member of the State Church, and officials of high rank in the government and teachers in universities and public schools also had to hold membership in the State Church. No person could withdraw from the State Church without entering another religious group, and since there was only one State Church in Sweden, a member withdrawing from it had to enter a church which was characterized by Swedish law as "*frammande trosbckannare,*" meaning "alien confession of faith."

Because of this monopoly by the State Church the pioneer Methodists, holding to Free Church principles, faced persecution. When the preachers began to hold public religious services, the State Church officials protested to the secular authorities, and this led to the arrest and punishment of some Methodist preachers. For example, when Johannes Nilsson preached at Varberg in 1871, he was fined one hundred and fifty kronors and placed in prison for eleven days on a diet of bread and water. Another preacher was fined a similar large amount for performing a marriage ceremony. On November 15, 1948, Bishop Theodor Arvidson participated in the eightieth jubilee celebration of Methodism at Kalmar. He was the guest of the governor, who was the son of a Methodist preacher, and a liberal Swedish newspaper pointed out that this incident showed some progress, for it was at Kalmar, years ago, that a Methodist had been met in the dark by a mob and had been slain.

The sufferings of Methodists reached such proportions that they appealed directly to the king of Sweden for relief. Through his aid, the Dissenter's Law of 1873 removed some of the most severe restrictions upon members of Free Churches.

Even today the Methodists do not have full freedom and equality. For many years all citizens were required to pay taxes for the support of the State Church, but a concession has recently been made for members of the Free Churches. Methodist preachers and laymen pay only one-half of the State Church tax if they present a statement of good standing from their local congregation.

THE METHODISTS OF CONTINENTAL EUROPE

The rule is still in force, however, by which high government officials and teachers must be members of the State Church, and Methodists must transfer to the State Church in order to hold such positions.

The absurdity of compelling a member who withdraws from the State Church to enter immediately another church in order to secure his certificate of withdrawal is shown by a recent example. A prominent labor leader in Sweden, holding atheistic views, desired to withdraw not only from the State Church but from all religious affiliations. His certificate of dismissal was denied, however, unless he would designate the church which he would join. In order to secure the certificate he said he was entering the Methodist Church, which of course he did not do, since he had disavowed all religion. Later this same man became prime minister of Sweden. He could not, however, take office, since he was listed as a Methodist on the government records. Then, in order to secure his new political position, he disavowed Methodism, of which he had never been a member, and was received again into the State Church.

NORWAY

In Norway, as in Sweden, all citizens were regarded as members of the State Church, which was supported by taxation. Certain types of employment, including teaching in elementary and secondary schools, were open only to members of the State Church. It meant loss of employment to become a Methodist. M. Hansen, a Methodist preacher, wrote in 1878: "No person that leaves the State Church can get or hold any office in the state; he cannot be an officer in the army or navy; he cannot be a judge; he cannot be a salesman or an apothecary, and so on."

When Methodism entered Norway it was at once attacked by the State Church as an heretical movement. Some leaders objected to its emphasis upon such doctrines as the witness of the Spirit and sanctification, and others declared that it was an insult to send Methodist missionaries to such an enlightened nation as Norway. There were attacks by the State Church press on Methodism and on several occasions the opposition led to violence. Dr. J. M. Reid has declared: "The Methodists were looked upon as a low and despised people and the State Church and its priests left nothing untried that could annoy or hinder them." By law no State Church pastor could give a certificate of withdrawal to any person under nineteen years of age, and this tended to block normal youth activities on the part of Methodism.

Denmark

In Denmark, also, there was much hostility to pioneer Methodism by the State Church. Its periodicals especially attacked Methodism. Several of the first preachers were persecuted, and in some places the stores refused to sell food to them.

Although the Methodists were given quasi-recognition in Denmark in 1886, certain restrictions remained. Methodist preachers had to be recognized individually by the government for each specified place of service, and this hindered general evangelistic work. All outdoor services were forbidden. By the law of 1886, however, Methodist ministers could solemnize marriage, bury their members in state cemeteries with the Methodist ritual, and keep official church records. But the Lutheran Church remained as the State Church of Denmark, with special privileges.

Finland

When the pioneer Methodists began to preach in Finland, they and their converts were persecuted. In one city all the tracts and books which had been distributed by their colporteurs were gathered and burned in the public square. The meetings of these "heretics" were disturbed by mobs. It was not until 1889 that Methodism was officially recognized in Finland. Five times before that date the Methodist ministers had been prohibited to preach, but, as one of them said: "We continued the work by the help of God."

Attacks upon Methodists continued into the modern period, as is shown by the experiences of Karl Hurtig, leader of Finnish

Methodism from 1904 to 1943. He was many times brought before the civil authorities on charges made by State Church pastors, one such charge being that he had performed marriage and burial services for non-Methodists and had baptized children whose parents were not Methodists.

GERMANY

The Protestant State Churches in the various territorial divisions of Germany refused to accept Methodism as a sister church and all official attempts by the Methodists to secure fraternal relations were for many years rejected. At a State Church conference held at Eisenach in 1855, a resolution was adopted declaring that any Protestant group other than a State Church was a "sect."

People were warned by State Church pastors to beware of Methodists. Pamphlets accused the Methodists of heresy and evil practices, and in press and pulpit they were attacked for upsetting the established ecclesiastical order by their religious enthusiasm. As late as 1887, a clergyman of the State Church in Thum issued the following statement: "It is correctly said . . . concerning the Methodists who are penetrating into Germany that they create the spirit of discord, the soul of rebellion, of arrogance, and of disintegration within Christianity to the confusion of the conscience. In short, the Methodist actions are what the Lord cited as the sin of the Pharisee (Matthew 23:15) : for spiritual arrogance makes one into a child of hell."

After Bishop John L. Nuelsen had examined hundreds of magistrate records in Saxony relating to legal actions against the Methodists, he declared that the state, the pulpit and the schools had united to fight them. He then added: "Are there not in our age, saturated with unholiness at the end of the nineteenth century, other powers which one ought to make war against than that little group of order-loving, peaceful citizens whose only crime consists in their desire to serve their God according to their best knowledge and conscience?" It was only in the Grand Duchy of Oldenburg and in Bremen and other Free Cities that the early Methodists had full liberty to preach and form congregations.

The Methodist preachers, because they insisted upon the right to proclaim the Gospel, suffered many indignities and persecutions. The experiences of Erhardt and Friedrick Wunderlich, founders of Methodism in Saxony, are typical. While Erhardt Wunderlich was holding family worship in a home at Dittersdorf, the police raided the house and, finding a Bible and hymnal on the table, arrested Wunderlich for conducting public worship. His brother, Friedrick Wunderlich, was fined many times for violating the law prohibiting preaching by "sectarians." Once when he refused to pay the fine, his cows were seized and sold at public auction to meet the payment. Another leader was fined in Saxony because he read the Bible and told a Bible story to a group of children; for this he was fined $7.50, and an additional $3.00 because he did not make payment immediately. In Berlin, a Methodist preacher was fined $25 and $15 in costs because he had met with some members at unauthorized hours in order to sing hymns. Since some of the early preachers had become naturalized in America they were not subject to arrest in Germany, but they were deported as undesirable visitors who were violating the religious laws.

The legal restrictions affected almost every phase of Methodist activity. Methodists and other Free Church members had to be buried in Saxony before 7:00 A.M., and there could be no funeral sermon by a Methodist preacher. Bishop J. W. E. Sommer points out that only fifteen years ago a Methodist preacher was fined ten marks for conducting a funeral service in a community cemetery near Rothenbergen. The charges were filed by a State Church pastor and the sentence was based upon an obsolete law of 1862.

Despite such hostile legislation, the pioneer Methodists found ways to hold religious services. In some places they held "tea meetings," during which religion was the only topic of conversation. Preachers were announced to give lectures and addresses instead of sermons. In Saxony the officials permitted the Methodists to have "lectures" in connection with worship in a home, subject to police approval for each "lecture."

There are examples of physical violence against the German Methodists. Mobs broke up their services, and, as in England in the eighteenth century, the police seldom interfered. At Vegesack a mob stoned the building in which the Methodists were worshipping until every window pane was broken. Louis Nippert and his colporteur, C. Nahrman, were met by a mob at Brunswick; they were physically assailed, the colporteur was beaten and thrown into a ditch, while Nippert was warned never to return to that place.

Some Methodist leaders, like Erhardt Wunderlich, despairing of obtaining religious freedom in Germany, returned to America. The treatment of Methodists in Hanover was so severe that Louis Nippert once wrote: "Our members who live there are suppressed and tyrannized. . . . If they desire to continue to serve God according to the convictions of their conscience, they have no other choice than to migrate to America."

SWITZERLAND

Even in democratic and freedom-loving Switzerland the Methodists suffered some persecution. Although the typical Swiss believes in religious freedom, the pastors of the State Churches appealed to Swiss law and tradition against the early Methodists.

From a legal standpoint the pastors insisted that all persons except Roman Catholics and Jews belonged to the State Churches, which, they asserted, supplied adequate religious facilities for all Protestants. A Methodist preacher was therefore looked upon and described as a wolf stealing sheep from the State Churchfold. Methodism was denied the status of a church and was publicly stigmatized as a sect of fanatical peasants.

The appeal to tradition stressed the fact that it was an insult for a missionary to come to a country which three centuries before had produced the Protestant Reformation under Huldreich Zwingli and John Calvin. The leaders pointed to the many cathedrals as proof of Swiss religion, and they were able for a short time to convince many Swiss people that Methodism upset honored Swiss traditions.

The situation was aggravated by the strict moral code of the Methodists. They did not remain behind closed doors but went into the streets with their message. The preachers were perfectionists and in no uncertain terms denounced sinners. No Swiss citizen enjoyed hearing his village described as a center of sin and that his salvation depended not upon membership in a church but on repentance from sin and personal acceptance of Jesus Christ. The result was persecution. Preachers were fined for preaching in the open air, and for twenty years they were mistreated by Swiss mobs.

To the credit of the Swiss people, defenders arose among liberal leaders, who, while denying the validity of the Methodist message, supported the Methodists on the ground of the traditional freedom of speech. It was not, however, until after World War I that the State Churches stopped describing Methodism as a sect. Even today an intricate process is necessary in certain Swiss cantons in order to withdraw officially from the State Church, and as a result many Swiss Methodists have a double church membership.

AUSTRIA

Let us now turn to the Catholic-dominated countries, beginning with Austria.

From 1870 to 1945 the Methodists were persecuted in Austria, a country often called the home of the Counter-Reformation, which enacted legislation to prevent the rise and growth of Protestantism.

The first Methodist pastor in Vienna labored for five years without being able to hold a public religious service. Methodism by law was restricted to "home worship." Servants could not even attend family prayers, for their presence would change the private devotions into public religious worship. One Methodist pastor was arrested, fined, and put in prison because he had read the Bible to children in his own home and had sung and prayed with them.

When Austrian Methodism finally dared to hold public services the police were present at the meetings. To avoid violating the laws, the Methodists were compelled to place notices on their halls in Vienna: "Admittance Only For Invited Guests," meaning only persons who could show a personal letter or card of invitation.

Another method was to invite people to attend "family Song Services."

These hindrances did not end with the nineteenth century. In 1928 Bishop John L. Nuelsen wrote: "While there is no longer an appeal to external force, as was customary under the old regime, a close watch is kept on all those who attend Methodist services. Parents are intimidated and children are discriminated against in the public schools by their Catholic teachers."

Roman Catholic attacks upon Protestantism in Austria came to a climax during the reactionary regimes between 1934 and 1938, when an attempt was made to make Austria a "true Catholic" state. A law was passed which provided for a medical examination of any convert to Protestantism in order to ascertain his mental condition. An interval of three months was required between application for Protestant membership and induction, in order that Roman Catholic pressure might be exerted upon the applicant. Preachers could be fined for expressing other than standard Roman Catholic opinion upon political events.

ITALY

Methodism in Italy was severely attacked by Roman Catholics. The Methodists were described in pamphlets as being atheistic, immoral and retrogressive, and the priests in sermons appealed to the national spirit by asserting that only Roman Catholics could be loyal Italians.

Roman Catholics were warned not to have any contact with the Methodists. The Bishop of Patenzia in 1873 threatened to excommunicate any person who attended Methodist services or schools. Teachers in some Italian schools told the children that they would not be advanced to higher classes if they went to Methodist Sunday Schools. In one Italian city the priests placed near the altar a large placard on which were written the names of those who entered Methodist places of worship; according to the placard, these persons had rendered themselves unfit to associate with Roman Catholics. As late as 1928 priests in Naples preached a special crusade against the Methodist orphanage, Casa Materna, and a special indulgence was promised to any Roman Catholic who succeded in taking children away from the institution. To become a Methodist usually meant the loss of secular employment.

Attacks in the press and from the altar led to mob violence. Superintendent Emanuele Sbaffi, referring to the early days of Methodism in Italy, has said: "Methodist ministers and congregations were often attacked by fanatic people, incited by priests, and several chapels were invaded, damaged or destroyed." Colporteurs were mobbed and their books were destroyed. Processions, often led by priests, paused before Methodist chapels and by noise made impossible the continuing of the Methodist service.

Secular officials, under clerical control, often blocked the rental or purchase of property by the Methodists, a policy which has even been followed in the twentieth century. In 1930 the Methodists built a chapel at Villa S. Sebastiano. When it was completed the Italian government forbade the Methodists to open it for public services, and for fourteen years the congregation of three hundred members was compelled to meet in the basement of their own building.

POLAND

The constitution adopted by the new republic of Poland at the close of World War I guaranteed religious freedom, but this was not always enforced. Poland between 1918 and 1939 was under the influence of the Roman Catholic hierarchy, and this ecclesiastical group was responsible for the bitter persecution of Methodists. Priests attacked Methodism as a foreign sect and appealed to nationalism by declaring that a loyal Pole could only be a Roman Catholic.

Many obstacles were encountered by Methodist workers. Inspired by priests, Polish mobs interrupted Methodist services. Miss Sallie Lewis Browne, on her first Sunday as a missionary at Wilno, in September, 1927, witnessed the breaking up of the Methodist meeting by a mob which tore up the hymnals and Bibles, broke the organ, and drove the worshippers from the hall. Konstanty

Najder, after an interrupted meeting in Ostrow in April, 1930, wrote: "Because of the assaults of the Romanists it was interrupted. I was flogged and our friends dispersed." As late as 1932, another pastor, Theodore Grabinski, was sentenced to one month in prison for publicly denying the divinity of the Virgin Mary.

Special attacks were made upon Methodist orphanages. Under clerical influence police officials raided the Methodist Orphanage at Odolanow in 1924, took away the fifty boys by force, and distributed them as servants in Roman Catholic homes, but within twenty-four hours the boys had escaped and returned to the orphanage. This incident, because of the unfavorable reaction in the foreign press, forced the officials at Warsaw to intervene to protect this orphanage. But the Methodist Orphanage at Pustomyty was closed because it had forty-three acres of land. According to law no benevolent agency could own more than forty acres, and the government refused to permit the orphanage to sell or give away the extra three acres in order to comply with the law.

Because of Roman Catholic influence, official recognition was denied Methodism in Poland prior to World War II. From a legal standpoint there was no Methodist Church in Poland. In order to hold property the Methodists were forced to organize a commercial corporation known as the Southern Trading Corporation, and to carry on educational work a separate Cultural Society was founded. As late as 1938 an official order was issued dissolving the Cultural Society and confiscating Methodist property. Prompt protest on the part of Southern Methodist Board of Missions and publicity in the American press forced the Polish authorities on the eve of World War II to rescind the order.

Ancient laws were revived to harass the Methodists. Because of legislation forbidding Protestant clergymen to minister to persons outside of their constituency, Methodist evangelistic meetings were hindered. Police often entered the halls and required each attendant to show a membership card. Methodist pastors could not baptize or perform marriage ceremonies, and since birth certificates based upon baptism were required, Methodist parents were compelled to have their children baptized by Lutheran or Reformed clergymen, who represented the two recognized Protestant State Churches in Poland.

In view of the continued persecution from 1922 to 1939 it is remarkable that Polish Methodism made any progress. Great tribute must be given to the small group of missionaries and the first generation of native Polish pastors who guided the church during those difficult years.

SPAIN

The persecution of the Methodists in Spain has been related by Franklin Albricias, son of Francisco Albricias, founder of the Model School at Alicante. He has written as follows: "In Alicante, as soon as the public Protestant meetings began and the number of pupils in the Model School increased, the attacks started, numerous and varied. Press campaigns of lies and calumnies were carried on against the Protestant school, the Reformation, Martin Luther, the Protestant countries and personally against my father. The greatest attacks against the Protestants in general and those of Alicante in particular were launched, violently and venomously, from the Catholic pulpit, especially during Lent. It would not be possible to say how many times the children in the school yard were stoned during play time, nor how many tiles and panes were broken. Once a heavy butcher's knife was thrown over the top of the wall surrounding the yard, falling among the boys. Several times my father was approached with magnificent offers if he would go back to the Roman Catholic Church. Menaces of every kind fell upon the Albricias family, in the columns of the papers, by telephone and by anonymous letters. More serious were two attempts to poison my father. This almost succeeded, and though he recovered, his health was impaired till his death. The other was an attempt to kidnap my brother Lincoln, then ten years old. Here the police had to interfere. Many, many times the enrollment of a child in the Model School led to the parent's loss of employment and the family's ostracism."

CZECHOSLOVAKIA

The Roman Catholics in Czechoslovakia were as violent in their hostility to Methodism as in other countries, but during the democratic regimes of President Thomas G. Masaryk and President Eduard Benes (1918-1938) they lacked the support of the government. Religious freedom was granted until the occupation by the Nazis in 1939.

Map of Czechoslovakia, showing principal centers of Methodist Work

Roman Catholic leaders, lacking political power, could only hinder Methodism by verbal attacks. The priests, hoping to arouse animosity against the Methodists from all groups in Czechoslovakia, charged the Methodists with being both Bolsheviks and also agents for American capitalism. When ten per cent of the population of Straz became Methodists, the bishop ordered the priests to use all and any means to curtail the movement. The priest at Lomnice punished the children for attending Methodist evangelistic services held in a tent, which he described as a "pig stall." The lack of political support however made such attacks largely impotent.

BELGIUM

The situation in Belgium was almost identical with that in Czechoslovakia. Roman Catholic leaders attacked Methodism in the press and from the pulpit, but although the large majority of Belgians were Roman Catholics, the government maintained a policy of religious neutrality. Religious instruction in the Belgian schools is provided by the state, and separate courses are provided, if demanded, for Protestant children. Under this plan Methodist pastors after 1930 were permitted to teach religion in the public schools.

HUNGARY

Although the Hungarian constitution guaranteed religious freedom, yet the early Methodists suffered some persecution and the Church was denied legal status until November, 1947. Many times the Methodist preachers were arrested and imprisoned. Upon appeal to the government authorities at Budapest these sentences were usually annulled, but for many years it was dangerous to hold Methodist services in isolated villages, where mobs often attacked the houses in which the services were held.

RUSSIA

We turn now to the Orthodox countries of Russia, Bulgaria and Yugoslavia.

Methodism was never regarded as a threat by the Orthodox Church in Russia. One reason was that the Methodist movement was never strong, except in the territory which later became the Baltic States of Latvia, Estonia and Lithuania. In Russia proper the greater part of the Methodist program was with foreign groups rather than with Russian citizens. Any great activity on the part of the Methodists among those who were members of the Orthodox Church would, however, have led to persecution. When Methodism entered Russia there was a law which forbade members of the Orthodox Church to renounce their faith, the penalty being detention for life in a convent prison. After the

Bolshevist Revolution of 1917 Methodists suffered persecution from the Communists.

BULGARIA

The Orthodox Church had played an important role in securing independence for Bulgaria from the Turks. It was, therefore, closely affiliated with the state and claimed a monopoly on religious affairs. It appealed to the aggressive Bulgarian national spirit in attacking all foreign churches. The Orthodox leaders asserted that a Bulgarian who left the Orthodox Church was a traitor to his country and had renounced his nationality.

Methodism was opposed vigorously by the Orthodox leaders and was assailed and slandered in the press. Priests visited from home to home, threatening to anathematize any who attended Methodist meetings, and many Bulgarians hesitated to attend for fear of arrest by the police. Until 1878 proselyting was forbidden by law in Bulgaria.

As late as 1889 the Exarch of Bulgaria endeavored to block further expansion of Methodism or any Protestant group. In this he had the support of the state officials. For a period no foreigner could teach in any school in Bulgaria; and no Protestant books could be given or sold to prisoners and soldiers. Bishop John L. Nuelsen once declared that no Bulgarian could join with the Methodists "without sooner or later going through the fire."

YUGOSLAVIA

In Yugoslavia also the Orthodox Church looked with disfavor upon the Methodists, and it was supported by the new national spirit of Yugoslavia after World War I. In 1928 Bishop John L. Nuelsen reported that Methodism, because its work was in those areas which formerly belonged to other nations, was closely watched, "especially since the Europeans, particularly those in the East, identify church and nationality and are accustomed to look upon the church as an agency to further nationalistic aspirations and aims. . . . Some of the minor officials seem still to regard the

Methodists as a sort of obscure dubious 'sect,' the real aims of which are not obvious." The School for Girls at Novi Sad was closed in 1929 by the government on the ground that it was a proselyting agency.

In regard to the attitude of the Orthodox Church, Superintendent Janos Tessenyi declared in 1924: "Hundreds of people come to hear the Gospel. But the priests are in fearful opposition as soon as one of the converts dares to join our church. The so-called 'historical' churches enjoy the special protection of the state and the priests use even the police in certain cases." Tessenyi held that it was only the smallness of Methodism in Yugoslavia that prevented severe persecution.

It was not until 1936 that Methodist pastors were permitted to perform marriage ceremonies. Since civil marriages were not recognized, the Methodist young people, according to Bishop John L. Nuelsen, had no choice until then "but to be married by an Orthodox priest who in that case claimed them and their children as members of his church, or to live together without the sanction of legal marriage."

Conclusion

In view of the persecutions which Methodists have suffered in Europe, it can be better understood why the church's membership has always been relatively small. This has not been due entirely to the persecution that was involved, however, but also to the difficulty of withdrawing from the State Churches, to which all citizens were by law supposed to be members from their birth.

In contrast to the freedom of personal choice of church membership, such as exists in America, an intricate legal process was required to withdraw from a State Church in order to join another. The individual had to make a personal application to the pastor or priest, and months would often elapse before an answer was given, during which time pressure was placed upon the applicant to change his views. If the certificate of withdrawal was granted by the State Church officials, the member then had to secure approval of a government official and pay a certain fee, the amount depending upon the number of persons in the family of the applicant. In most countries no person could, even by this process, change his religious affiliation before reaching the age of eighteen.

The regulations in Hungary provide a typical example of how difficult it has been to become a Methodist in Europe. A baptismal certificate was required for nearly every legal process in Hungary, and to enroll in schools or secure passports. Since Methodism was not officially recognized until 1947, its pastors could not issue baptismal certificates to their own members. Methodists were listed on public documents as having "no religion," since Methodism was not officially recognized, and the statement "no religion" was then interpreted as meaning that the person involved was a Communist and subject to police supervision. Prior to World War II children could not be promoted to higher classes in public schools without a satisfactory grade in religion, attested by an official of one of the State Churches. Since the Methodist Sunday School was not recognized, Methodist preachers were forced to send their own children to State Church pastors or priests for religious instruction in order to secure their advancement in public school studies.

It is not surprising that in Europe many people have remained as Methodist adherents or sympathizers instead of becoming members. The Methodist constituency has always been at least three times larger than the actual membership.

DISCUSSION SUGGESTIONS

1. What are the essential principles and the main points of difference between the Roman Catholic Church, the Orthodox Church, and the Protestant State Churches? In what countries are each strong? Note the fact that each is a "State Church."

2. Describe the manner in which the Roman Catholic Church persecuted the Methodists?

3. Describe the persecutions from the Orthodox Church.

4. Describe the persecutions from the Protestant State Churches.

Switzerland, showing principal centers of Methodist work

CHAPTER IV

FROM 1914 TO 1939

EUROPEAN Methodism was seriously affected by World War I (1914-1918), since half of the members lived in the belligerent countries. It is estimated that five thousand Methodist laymen were in military service, and that ten per cent of these were killed in battle. Nearly two hundred Methodist preachers were drafted into military service. One-third of the German preachers were in uniform and nearly all the preachers in Austria-Hungary were called to arms, there being at one time only one pastor able to continue his work in southern Hungary. In Italy one district superintendent, two theological professors, and one-third of the pastors served in the Italian army. The absence of the pastors from their charges resulted in a temporary decline in Methodism in some communities.

Bishop John L. Nuelsen remained nobly at his post of duty in Europe during the entire war. Until America entered the war in April, 1917, he was able to go into all the European countries except Russia, and he went into the war zones and visited military hospitals and prisoner-of-war camps. Bishop Nuelsen has been described as the instrument in European Methodism during those years through which faith and brotherhood were maintained despite the animosities and devastation of the war. He proved a stabilizing force in all parts of the church.

The close of the war in November, 1918, left the belligerent nations of Europe depleted and their citizens in great need of relief. One of the brightest chapters in Methodist history is the story of Methodist relief and reconstruction in war-torn Europe after 1918. All branches of American Methodism made generous gifts of funds and supplies. Methodist relief work for Poland, Belgium and Czechoslovakia, assigned to Southern Methodism, was under the guidance of Bishop W. B. Beauchamp, with headquarters in Brussels, Prague and Warsaw. Relief work for the other European nations was sponsored by the Methodist Episcopal Church under the leadership of Bishop Nuelsen at Zurich, Switzerland. In addition to the gifts from America, the Swiss and Scandinavian Methodists made generous and sacrificial contributions, and many millions of dollars were expended in this humanitarian service.

Among the many forms of Methodist relief was the care of destitute children. As early as 1919 orphans and needy children of Austria and Germany were brought to Switzerland, Denmark, Sweden and Norway. In addition Bishop Nuelsen founded institutional homes for needy children in Austria, Hungary and Germany. In 1925 ten thousand children were being cared for in these Methodist institutions.

Bishop Nuelsen considered the condition of European children to be the most serious problem of post-war Europe. He wrote in 1920: "Today I am haunted by the sight of thousands of pale, hollow-eyed, careworn, hunger-pinched faces of mothers and maidens; by the sight of emaciated, half-dressed, weak, sickly, subnormal children . . . all over Europe, thousands of them, hundreds of thousands, millions. Draw a line through the devastated areas of Belgium and France from north to south, go eastward through Germany, Switzerland, Italy into Austria, Hungary, Serbia, Albania, Czechoslovakia, Poland, farther east through the Balkan states, and Russia, clear through to Siberia and the Indian Ocean, and you will find hardly one child in a thousand that is normal, physically or intellectually or morally." Prophetically he asked in 1920: "What is to become of Europe if we allow a whole generation to grow up physically, intellectually, morally subnormal, not able to grapple with the problem which will confront European society thirty years from now?"

THE MISSIONARY CENTENARY

European Methodism at the close of World War I was also helped by the Missionary Centenary celebration of 1919 which marked the one hundredth anniversary of the first Missionary Society of American Methodism. During the Centenary period American Methodists subscribed more than one hundred million dollars to be used in home and foreign fields and in the reconstruction of Methodism in war-torn countries. Liberal donations from these funds were made to European Methodism and made possible not only the repairing of war-damaged property but also a marked advance in the building of churches, schools and other Methodist institutions.

There were, however, some unfavorable results for European Methodists of the Centenary movement. The sudden shrinking of Centenary funds after 1923 made impossible the completion of some Centenary projects that had been started and left large debts in several annual conferences. The loss of Centenary funds coincided with the post-war economic depression in Europe, and the local churches were unable to assume extra financial burdens.

THE DEPRESSION

After 1923 the income for foreign missionary work of both Northern and Southern Methodism in America was lowered and radical cuts were made in the appropriations to European fields. These cuts reached serious proportions. For example, the Zurich Area, under the supervision of Bishop Nuelsen, received in 1926 only one-fourth as much in appropriations as it had been granted in 1921. The financial depression struck America in 1929, and further radical cuts had to be made in the support of European Methodism.

Methodist work in Europe suffered seriously during the period of these economic depressions, which became international in scope. As early as 1926 Bishop Nuelsen was forced to write as follows concerning the curtailment of work in the Balkan countries: "We dismissed most of our supplies; we discontinued some appointments; we scaled down expenses everywhere." Building projects were stopped, and in some countries the theological students were advised to leave their studies, since there seemed to be no hope of future employment for pastors. Bishop Raymond J. Wade, in referring to the adverse effect of the lowering of missionary appropriations for the Baltic and Slavic Annual Conference, said in 1932: "Our pastors live on starvation wages. Children have died in our parsonage homes because of insufficient nourishment." The financial depressions also had serious results for the young Methodist churches in Belgium, Czechoslovakia and Poland, and by 1933 it was necessary to recall most of the American missionaries from these three countries.

Despite the difficult economic features, the depression period was also one of the noblest eras in European Methodism. It clearly demonstrated that the church was not dependent upon financial support from America. It was a great testing period, and from this experience there came a stronger European Church. Dr. J. P. Bartak, reminiscing about this period, has written: "Our preachers accepted their lot under the pressure of the crisis. It is remarkable what people can endure and what sacrifices preachers are capable of making when they are asked to endure for the great and noble cause which they represent."

To the honor of the European Methodists, they refused to allow the economic difficulties to keep them from working toward their goal of self-support. Prior to World War I steps had been taken toward this end, but it was delayed by the outbreak of the war. Now, even in the darkest days of economic depression, the older sections of European Methodism advanced toward their aim of self-support. This was attained in Switzerland in 1931. All the annual conferences in Germany and Sweden were self-supporting by 1936. The same goal was attained by the Norwegian and Danish Methodists in 1938.

It should always be remembered that the gifts from America to European Methodism have never been large. In 1939 Bishop Nuelsen declared that, except in the beginning of a work and in periods of reconstruction after wars, "the great bulk of millions of dollars invested in houses of worship, church buildings, parsonages, hospitals, homes, publishing houses does not come from sources in America but represents the sacrificial giving of the

European membership." He further declared that because of this policy European Methodism had not become a foreign ecclesiastical colony but an indigenous church, "a part of the life of the nations, nourished by the lifeblood of the people."

In order to understand better the progress of European Methodism from the close of World War I in 1918 and the beginning of World War II in 1939 a brief account is given of the work in the various countries during that period.

SCANDINAVIAN COUNTRIES

The Scandinavian Methodists made large contributions for the relief of needy Methodists in the war-torn nations. Bishop Nuelsen wrote in 1920: "Our Scandinavian brethren have also taken their share in carrying the burden of starving Europe. They opened their homes to underfed children from Vienna and Germany even at a time when political feeling ran quite high; they sent money, food, clothing across the Baltic Sea to those that are in dire need."

A most constructive development in Scandinavian Methodism was the founding in 1924 of the Union Scandinavian School of Theology at Gothenburg, Sweden. From the beginning each national group in the Scandinavian countries had maintained a theological seminary, but there was need for a school for advanced studies. This could only be made possible through the cooperation of all the Scandinavian Methodists, which became a reality with the establishment of the new school at Gothenburg. By 1935 fifty Methodist preachers from Sweden and thirty from Norway, Denmark and Finland had been students in this school.

During this period much progress was made toward self-support and autonomy. The growth of Scandinavian Methodism was evidenced when one of its leaders, Anton Bast of Denmark, was elected bishop by the General Conference of 1920. By 1924 the annual conferences in the Scandinavian countries became the Northern Europe Central Conference. In 1938 Scandinavian Methodists, with the exception of Finland and the Baltic States, had become self-supporting.

There was also an increased missionary activity, and the contribution to foreign missions far exceeded the financial assistance received by the Scandinavian Methodists from the American Church. In addition to liberal gifts for foreign missions, the Swedish Methodists in 1927 raised more than $50,000 for home missionary enterprises. In 1939 Scandinavian Methodists were serving as foreign missionaries in Sumatra, Belgian Congo, North Africa, Rhodesia, Southeast Africa, India, Korea, Portuguese East Africa, and Malaya. This remarkable record caused Dr. R. E. Diffendorfer to assert: "Nothing so attests the vitality of Scandinavian Methodism as its world-wide missionary interest."

The social service program, especially deaconess work, was increased between 1914 and 1939. In 1915 the Swedish Methodists founded a Deaconess Hospital for mental diseases at Gothenburg, and in 1926 they started a Deaconess Training School which had the approval of the Swedish government for the training of nurses. A Deaconess Hospital and Home was established in Stockholm in 1932. A modern hospital at Skien was erected in 1939 by the Norwegian Methodists. The central Mission at Copenhagen, directed by Danish Methodists, became recognized as being among the best social service agencies in any continental country.

From 1928 until 1940 the superintendent of the Scandinavian work was Bishop Raymond J. Wade, the first resident bishop in Stockholm. His friendly and brotherly spirit plus his wise leadership did much toward making Scandinavian Methodism ready for complete autonomy.

GERMANY

Despite losses during World War I and the sufferings of the post-war financial depressions, Methodism in Germany made a phenomenal recovery. Through campaigns made by Bishop John L. Nuelsen and Dr. F. H. Otto Melle, especially among German-speaking Methodists in America, liberal financial assistance was secured. In 1926 the North Germany Annual Conference became self-supporting. The other four annual conferences soon attained the same goal and by 1936 German Methodism was receiving no missionary appropriations from America.

There was also a large gain in membership. Between 1918 and 1923 there was a growth of thirty per cent. In 1925 the number of annual conferences was increased from two to five. By 1939 there were 45,000 members in Germany, with two hundred and fifty ordained preachers and eight hundred lay preachers. Methodism also received recognition as a legal corporation and could hold property in the name of the church.

A most outstanding feature of German Methodism was the enlargement of the Theological Seminary at Frankfurt-am-Main. Under the presidency of Dr. F. H. Otto Melle, large gifts came from American Methodists for the Seminary. The securing of a good library and the faculty of six recognized scholars raised the prestige both of the Seminary and of German Methodism. In 1923 there were eighty-four students in the Seminary from nineteen European nations and from India, China and America. By 1939 almost all of the Methodist theological students from Germany, Switzerland, Austria, Hungary, Yugoslavia and Bulgaria were receiving their education at this Seminary.

By 1936 German Methodism was able to qualify as a separate Central Conference, with the right to elect its own bishop. When Bishop John L. Nuelsen opened the first Germany Central Conference in 1936 he said: "No longer can the Methodist Church in Germany be called an 'alien plant,' a colony of a foreign organization. The Methodist Episcopal Church in Germany is from now on exclusively under German leadership. German Methodists can look their national comrades in the eye and say, 'Methodism is German.' "

Dr. F. H. Otto Melle was elected as the first bishop of the Germany Central Conference. He had served in many capacities. He had been a missionary in Hungary and Yugoslavia, the leader of the anti-alcohol movement in Germany, president of the Theological Seminary at Frankfurt-am-Main from 1920 to 1936, and the leader of the Free Church Council in Germany.

The rise of National Socialism presented a serious problem for

Methodism as well as all other religious groups. Methodist youth societies were dissolved under the Nazi program of Adolf Hitler. In many ways the Methodists felt the pressure of the totalitarian Nazi system, but endeavored to adjust to the new situation without compromising principles. Bishop Melle wrote in 1939: "I am glad to report that the work of the Methodist Episcopal Church in Germany is going on in a hopeful way. That we—like the other Evangelical Free Churches—found a positive relation to the new state, that we kept neutral in the church-conflict, and that we confine our task, like Paul in Corinth, to knowing nothing but Christ and to preach his gospel, won the confidence of the government, made us known in the public, and gave us new opportunities."

SWITZERLAND

During and immediately after World War I Swiss Methodism made sacrificial gifts to the needy Methodists in war-torn countries, especially in Germany and Austria. Bishop Nuelsen reported in 1920 that the Swiss Methodists had "opened their homes to thousands of underfed children from Vienna, Germany, and Italy. They collected clothes and provisions and sent whatever they could spare to clothe and feed the naked and hungry." By 1924 the Swiss Methodists had collected and sent to suffering countries enough relief supplies to fill more than eighty freight cars.

The financial assistance given to Methodists in eastern Europe by the Swiss Methodists was very generous. Shortly after World War I Swiss laymen loaned large sums of money to Methodist churches and institutions in Germany, Austria, and Hungary. When, during the post-war financial depressions, the Austrian and Hungarian Methodists were unable to pay these debts, Swiss Methodism did something perhaps unparalleled in the annals of the church: the Methodist laymen relinquished one-third of their claims while the Switzerland Annual Conference, with the aid of Bishop Nuelsen, assumed the remaining two-thirds of the debts.

In 1933, Dr. and Mrs. Ferdinand Sigg made an extended official visit on behalf of Swiss Methodism to the Methodists of eastern

Europe. As a result of their report the Swiss Methodist Missionary Society came to the rescue of their needy brethren. Missionaries were sent to Yugoslavia while financial assistance was given to the Austrian and Hungarian Methodists. The Switzerland Annual Conference provided one building at the Methodist Social Center at Budakesci, Hungary. In 1936 Bishop Nuelsen declared that "we should have been compelled to abandon our work in those countries (Austria, Hungary and Yugoslavia) were it not for the support of the Swiss Methodists." In 1936 the Swiss Methodists were supporting seven missionaries in foreign countries.

Swiss Methodist laymen have played an important part in adjusting the social and labor problems of Switzerland. After World War I there was much industrial unrest and many workers were influenced by the teachings of Lenin, who had lived for two years as an exile in Switzerland. To combat these Communist influences there was founded the Christian Workman's Association, in which Methodist laymen have always been very active. The lay leader of Swiss Methodism, Dr. Gottfried Frei, was among the founders of the Association. For many years the president of the Association has been Emanuel Bangerter, a Methodist layman of St. Gallen.

There were many other encouraging features in Swiss Methodism between 1914 and 1939. With the assistance of Centenary funds a large building program was started. In 1922 the Methodist Church was admitted as a member of the Swiss Church Federation, being the first Free Church admitted on equal standing with the Swiss State Churches. In 1931 Swiss Methodism became self-supporting.

Austria

The dissolution of Austria-Hungary in 1918 necessitated a change in Methodist administration, and the Austria-Hungary Mission Conference gave way to three separate Mission Conferences in Austria, Hungary, and Yugoslavia.

As in Germany, a large relief program was adopted for Austrian Methodism after the close of World War I. Its outstanding feature was the founding in 1923 of "Auhof" in Turnitz, which by 1936 had cared for twenty-eight thousand children and adults for periods of from three weeks to three months. The work at Turnitz became so popular that in 1936 Bishop Nuelsen wrote: "We hope to make this Home both a center of wholesome influence and a revenue for other parts of our work."

With the founding of the new republic of Austria in 1918 religious freedom was promised to all citizens, and it seemed as if Methodism would make great progress. Bishop Nuelsen wrote in 1924 that Austria was "still an open country, the masses are hungry for the Gospel, large crowds attend the evangelistic services. We have many open doors. Our embarrassment is in the lack of equipment. In the city of Vienna we could open a mission in every one of the twenty-two districts into which the city is divided and would have it crowded with people if we had the means to rent or buy or build." This situation, however, was only temporary, for the Austrian Republic soon came under Roman Catholic control and one result was the persecution of the Methodists.

YUGOSLAVIA

In 1920 the Yugoslav Mission Conference became a part of the Paris Area, under the episcopal supervision of Bishop Edgar Blake, who gave special attention to Yugoslavia. Under his leadership, a hostel for young men and a clinic were opened in Belgrade. He also founded a School for Girls at Novi Sad. In 1921 the small orphanage at Srbroban was moved to Novi Sad and it had forty-five orphans in 1925.

In 1922 ten churches in Macedonia, formerly connected with the Bulgarian Congregational Church, were added to the Yugoslav Mission Conference. Political reasons made it impossible for a Bulgarian organization to work in Yugoslavia and at the request of the Congregational Church these congregations united with the Methodist Church in Yugoslavia.

The curtailment of Centenary funds affected the Methodist program in Yugoslavia, but other problems also arose. One difficulty was that Methodism worked in Yugoslavia with minority groups, the Germans and Hungarians in the northern part and the Macedonians in southern Yugoslavia. Methodism never made much progress with the Serbs, Croats, and Slovenes who represented the majority of Yugoslav citizens. The School for Girls at Novi Sad was closed in 1929 because of the refusal of the government to permit foreign schools to operate. The school was then made, with the assistance of Swiss Methodists, into a sanatorium which in 1936 was one of the two Protestant hospitals in Yugoslavia.

HUNGARY

The close of World War I found Hungarian Methodism in very difficult circumstances and much relief assistance was necessary. The care of war orphans led to the founding by Bishop Nuelsen of a Children's Home at Budakesci, which in 1931 was made into a Deaconess Sanatorium for the care of tubercular patients.

In 1924 Bishop Nuelsen was optimistic over the future of Hungarian Methodism. He wrote: "We have, in addition to our headquarters in Budapest, properties in three other places; we have a Book Concern, a preparatory seminary for preachers, an orphan home, a children's home located in Budakesci, a charming mountain resort, where we take care of more than two hundred underfed children from the slums of Budapest; we operate an industrial school for girls, and a day nursery for children in one of the most densely populated sections of the capital city; we manage a young men's home; we have started a temperance restaurant, the only one in the city of Budapest; we publish a temperance paper in the Hungarian language and are considered the leaders in the prohibition movement in the country. The story of our work in Hungary is a marvel. I question a better anywhere in the world; an investment of $5,000 per year is yielding large returns. But the appropriation is pitifully inadequate. With $15,000 to $20,000 a year we could revolutionize the religious life of the nation." Lack of adequate financial support after 1924, however, made impossible the continuation of a large Methodist program in Hungary.

BULGARIA

The brightest feature of Bulgarian Methodism between 1914 and 1939 was the American School for Girls at Lovetch, which was founded in 1882. During World War I it was closed for several years because of lack of food for the students, but it was reopened in 1920 and was given official recognition, which placed it on a par with state schools. In order to accommodate the large number of applicants for admission, two new buildings were erected in 1928. In that year Bishop John L. Nuelsen declared that the school had become a vital factor in the educational life of Bulgaria.

An attempt was made to unite the Methodists and Congregationalists in Bulgaria. Since these two groups had from their entrance into Bulgaria worked in close cooperation, there arose a desire for organic unity which would provide one strong Bulgarian Protestant Church. It is to be regretted that after fifteen years of negotiation the plan failed in 1938, because of the inability to adjust the different policies of the Methodists and Congregationalists concerning the holding of property.

RUSSIA

The triumph of Bolshevism and the anti-religious policy of the government after 1917 almost destroyed Methodism in Russia. In 1920 Bishop John L. Nuelsen made the following discouraging report: "What shall I say of distracted Russia? Dr. George A. Simons and his sister remained at their post in Petrograd, helping the distressed, comforting the dying, although daily confronted by personal suffering and in danger of life, as long as the American government permitted any American citizens to stay in the country. They were among the last Americans to leave Russia. . . . All efforts to get in touch with Sister Anna, our heroic deaconess, or others failed. Now, however, Dr. Simons brings word that our property is intact, that Sister Anna is living, doing as much good as she can, respected even by the Bolshevist rulers, but being compelled to sell one piece of furniture after another, one garment after another, in order to buy bread."

Dr. Simons, from his headquarters in Riga, Latvia, endeavored
for several years to continue the Methodist work in Russia.
Deaconess Anna Eklund remained in Russia until 1927 but by
1930 there were no Methodist leaders in that country.

THE BALTIC STATES

At the close of World War I the three Baltic States of Estonia,
Latvia, and Lithuania, formerly parts of Russia, became independ-
ent nations. Methodism had begun work in these states as early
as 1904, when they were still under Russian control. The Baltic
and Slavic Annual Conference was organized in 1929 with Estonian,
Latvian and Lithuanian districts. It was attached to the Stockholm
Area. In 1939 there were three thousand Methodists in the Baltic
States.

FRANCE

Immediately after the close of World War I much progress was
made in France. The Methodist churches in Strasbourg and Colmar
became a part of the French Annual Conference with the return
of Alsace-Lorraine to France. The heroic struggle of France
between 1914 and 1918 brought a renewed interest by the American
churches in French Methodism, and generous contributions of
Centenary funds made possible the execution of a large social
service program. At Charvieu a home and school was founded for
dependent boys, with a similar institution for girls at Champfleury.
A school for girls was started at Grenoble, and a social center was
organized at Chateau-Thierry. The Methodist Memorial in Paris
became the best known community center in France. A model
agricultural farm was operated at Charvieu. In 1920 Bishop Nuelsen
reported that formerly the Methodist Episcopal Church was hardly
known in France, but "now the name is known and respected all
over the country."

The shrinkage of Centenary funds and the reduction of missionary appropriations made impossible the continuance of this large
program. Since French Methodism was unable to adopt a policy of
self-support, it became necessary to disband the French Annual

Conference in 1935. The congregations in Alsace-Lorraine were then attached to the Switzerland Annual Conference. Most of the other Methodist congregations merged with the French Reformed Church, but six groups remained as independent Methodist churches. In regard to the closing of French Methodism Bishop Raymond J. Wade wrote in 1936: "Thus, inadvertently ended a chapter of our history just when the churches, tested as by fire and evangelistically inspired, were prepared to go forward to accomplish their real mission in this religiously needy country."

ITALY

Italian Methodism was not seriously affected by World War I, and with generous Centenary gifts after 1918 the Italian work reached large proportions. In 1921 there were forty-two preachers in the Italy Annual Conference, and there were churches and social centers in fifty Italian cities. Italian Methodism had the leading orphanage in Italy, and it operated notable educational institutions, such as the Collegio Internazionale at Monte Mario, Rome, Crandon International Institute at Rome, and an Industrial School at Venice. In addition there were in Rome a large headquarters building, a theological seminary, a publishing house, a dispensary, and a church for English-speaking people.

Dark days, however, soon came upon Italian Methodism. The sudden curtailment of Centenary funds and the decreased missionary appropriations incident to the post-war economic depressions seriously harmed the work and many churches and social institutions were forced to close their doors.

Of more serious nature, however, was the systematic attack by the Fascist leaders and the Vatican which followed the signing of the Concordat and the Lateran Pacts by Benito Mussolini and Pope Pius XI in 1929. The essence of these agreements is contained in the sentence: "Italy recognizes the Catholic religion as the sole religion of the State." It became illegal for Protestant groups to continue evangelistic work. Distribution of religious literature and personal discussions concerning religion, being considered as proselyting, became illegal acts. Pope Pius XI, in his joy over the new religious policy, praised Mussolini and declared: "There was need for a man like the one Providence sent us." The pope saw nothing unethical in making an alliance with Fascism in 1929.

The attack by the Vatican on Methodism coincided with the extreme nationalistic policy of Mussolini's Fascist regime. Since only Italian schools were permitted, the Methodists were forced to sell their educational institutions. In most cases the funds secured from the sales had to be invested in Italian state bonds, the income from which could be used only with the approval of the Italian authorities. Another decree required payment of large indemnities to all persons who were released from employment through the forced sale of the properties. Other Fascist legislation made it illegal for a "foreign" church to operate in Italy. It became necessary to set up an organization entirely separate from American Methodism, and the Italian Methodist Church was founded in 1935 with no organic relation to any other section of the ecumenical church.

On the eve of World War II the Vatican attempted to close the Methodist orphanage, Casa Materna, near Naples. The Fascist government, under Vatican pressure, decreed that this outstanding institution should be closed because it was not needed and because Protestant propaganda was made at Casa Materna. Superintendent Riccardo Santi appealed from this ruling to the Italian Supreme Court. This placed the court in an embarrassing situation, for there was no evidence to justify a decision against Casa Materna and yet the court feared to oppose the Vatican. The court therefore suggested that the decision be delayed, and in the meantime the orphanage should be closed. When Superintendent Santi replied that the state must then take care of the three hundred orphans in Casa Materna, it was decided that the orphanage could remain open until a final verdict was issued by the court. When the author met Superintendent Santi in Naples, in April, 1945, the latter said: "The decision came with the American soldiers."

Spain

Until 1936 much progress was made in Spanish Methodism. Before Francisco Albricias died in 1934, at the age of seventy-eight, he had seen the Model School reach an enrollment of one thousand students. Two of his sons, Lincoln and Franklin Abricias, became the leaders of Spanish Methodism after the death of their father. Franklin Albricias, who had been educated in Switzerland, became the superintendent of the Spanish Methodist Mission, while Lincoln, a layman, who had been educated at the University of Madrid, became the director of the Model School.

The revolution which began in 1936 under the leadership of General Francisco Franco proved fatal to the Model School and the Methodist congregations. The Franco regime, with the support of the Roman Catholic hierarchy, became violently anti-Protestant. Pastors and Protestant leaders were arrested and imprisoned. The situation became so desperate that in 1938 Franklin Albricias, as the representative of the Spanish Protestant Federation of Churches, made trips through France, Switzerland, Belgium and Holland, seeking financial assistance, food and clothing for the persecuted Protestants of his country. He was in Belgium when World War II began, and when the Nazis entered Belgium in May, 1940, he was forced to flee to France. It was not until 1941 that he and his family were able to find refuge with the Methodists in North Africa.

Lincoln Abricias remained in charge of the Model School at Alicante until the Franco regime came into complete control of Spain in 1939. Before leaving Alicante, Albricias placed a notice on the Model School stating that it was American property. This did not prove of any value, for when the Franco troops entered Alicante the school was seized and since that time the property has been used jointly by the Falangist Party and a religious order of the Roman Catholic Church. Lincoln Albricias and his family, as well as other Methodist laymen, were able to escape from Spain and go to North Africa.

MADEIRA ISLANDS

In 1933 an attempt was made to merge the Methodist and Scotch Presbyterian congregations on the Madeira Islands into the Evangelical Union. All financial support from American Methodism ceased, but the merger was not a complete success. Bishop Raymond J. Wade, commenting on the attempted union, aptly stated that "haste and compulsion make waste in mergers."

BELGIUM

Many Belgian people attended the Methodist evangelistic meetings, which were conducted first in tents, rented halls, and on the streets. Congregations were organized in the main centers of Belgium and special progress was made with the laboring classes. It was possible after 1922 to erect a large headquarters building in Brussels, a school and orphanage in Brussels, and with other Protestant groups to support a Protestant hospital there. A bookstore was established and the Molenbeek Church became noted for social service activities.

One important step was the relating of Belgian Methodism to the Methodist missionary work in the Belgian Congo. Young Belgian Methodists began to volunteer for missionary service in the Congo, and apartments were provided in the Methodist headquarters building in Brussels for missionaries from abroad who studied in Belgium before going to the African colony.

But Methodist work in Belgium was seriously affected by the post-war financial depression. In 1933 it was necessary to recall some of the missionaries. Financial support from America almost ceased for several years and it became necessary to sell some property in Belgium and close some institutions.

CZECHOSLOVAKIA

No European Methodist group began with greater promise of success than did the Czechoslovak Methodists. By 1926 there were already ten thousand members and adherents. Vrsovice Church in Prague was for a period the largest local congregation in the

Methodist Episcopal Church, South. Educational and social service institutions were founded after 1922, and in a short time the Czechoslovak Church had won a high place in public esteem.

One outstanding feature of Czechoslovak Methodism was the organization in 1924 of a society for the care of orphans. An orphanage was founded at Horni Pocernice and was supported entirely by Czechoslovak Methodists. Later an ancient castle at Tynec, in southwestern Bohemia, was acquired, and in this spacious building there was room not only for an orphanage but also a home for aged people. Tynec became the center for summer camps for children, youth activities, and Bible training schools.

It is to be regretted that the post-war financial depression deprived Czechoslovak Methodism of needed support at that high moment. As Dr. J. P. Bartak has written, the Czechoslovak Methodists "experienced shocks during the years 1931-1934 that were entirely out of the ordinary course of the regular missionary program." American missionaries were forced to return home and native pastors were dismissed for lack of funds to pay salaries.

POLAND

Despite severe persecution, Polish Methodism made progress between 1922 and 1939, especially in educational and social service institutions. In 1923 an English Language School was opened in Warsaw under Methodist auspices to meet the desires of numerous Poles to learn the English language. Outstanding people, rectors of academies, judges, physicians, diplomats and political officials enrolled in the school, and by 1939 there was an enrollment of eleven hundred students, ninety-five per cent of whom were Roman Catholics. Practically all of the citizens of Warsaw, including members of the government, who today speak English learned the language in this great Methodist school.

A second institution affecting the cultural life of Poland was the Methodist School at Klarysew, under the direction of a great Polish teacher and Methodist convert, Dr. Wladyslaw Dropiowski. By 1928 the best families of Poland were sending their children to the Klarysew School, the only Protestant boarding school in Poland. In 1927 the Methodist Bible School was founded in Warsaw and in 1930 three young men graduated, these being the first Methodist-trained Polish preachers.

As in other countries Polish Methodism was seriously hurt by the financial depressions between 1929 and 1935. Most of the missionaries were recalled in 1933, and it became necessary to discharge half of the native preachers and to close the Methodist School at Klarysew in the same year. But a remarkable recovery began in 1935 which overcame many of the losses of the depression period. Hardly had this started, however, when the invasion of Poland by the military forces of Adolf Hitler in September, 1939, created a new crisis in Polish Methodism.

DISCUSSION SUGGESTIONS

1. Discuss the effect of World War I on the Methodist churches of continental Europe.

2. Discuss the Missionary Centenary. Show how the Centenary funds made possible a great expansion of Methodism in France, Italy, and other countries, and its establishment in Belgium, Poland and Czechoslovakia.

3. Discuss the effect of the financial depressions on European Methodism. Show the effect country by country.

Germany, showing the more important of the 1,000 centers of Methodism

CHAPTER V

METHODISM IN WORLD WAR II

THE unity of European Methodism was evidenced by the holding of the All-European Methodist Conference at Copenhagen, Denmark, August 2-6, 1939, less than one month before the outbreak of World War II. It has been described as being probably the last large international gathering held on the continent prior to the beginning of hostilities. To the Copenhagen Conference went three hundred and twenty delegates from twenty countries representing one hundred and twelve thousand Methodists. Many church leaders from America were also present.

The Conference was held in an atmosphere of international tension, which was well expressed by Dr. J. P. Bartak of Czechoslovia, which had already been overrun by Hitler. He said: "We are living in a world that is constantly changing. If this meeting had been held one year ago I would have attended as a delegate from the Czechoslovak Republic and from the Methodist Episcopal Church, South. Today both of these entities have been rubbed out. My prayer at the beginning of this Conference is, 'O thou who changest not, abide with me.' " A silence fell upon the audience, and then the entire body stood in honor of the suffering Czechoslovak Methodists. The episcopal address at the Conference also referred to the political tension and asserted that the totalitarian claims of Jesus Christ, not those of dictators, constituted the answer of Methodism to the world's deep need.

There were many results of the Copenhagen Conference, of which the most important, perhaps, was the recognition of the unity of European Methodism, a unity which was not to be lost during the long years of World War II. It was possible to adopt a message by a unanimous vote, showing that on the eve of the war these Methodists were above nationalism.

Commenting on this meeting, Dr. R. E. Diffendorfer said: "The

Conference emphasized what we do not always remember, namely, that we have a vigorous Methodism on the continent of Europe. One important purpose of the Conference was to weld the Methodisms of the various continental nations into unity, to bring about the same consciousness of oneness as came out of the recent Uniting Conference at Kansas City. . . . We believe that Copenhagen produced a sense of brotherhood in a common cause which no war can eradicate. If any question whether or not Methodism has any real mission in Europe, the Copenhagen meeting answered it with unmistakable clarity. Methodism cannot escape its mission in Europe!"

Before some of the delegates could return to their homes, World War II had begun. An immediate test was therefore placed, not only upon the unity of Methodism in Europe, but also upon its ability to survive nearly six years of "total war" affecting directly the civilian population as well as the soldiers on the battlefields. The following brief account describes Methodist affairs in each of the European nations during the period of the war.

GERMANY

In 1948 Bishop J. W. E. Sommer gave the following account of the position of the German Methodists during the Hitler regime: "The last fifteen years have been the most trying in the history of Methodism in Germany, and I can say with conviction: 'We have kept the faith.' During all the propaganda of hate and dictatorial subjection of the individual conscience, we preached unabated the gospel of the love of Christ for all men and the eternal verities of God's unalterable commandments, and the infinite value of every human being. I, myself, said in a sermon in the Second Church at Frankfurt: 'If anyone forbid me to treat as a brother a Jew who has accepted Christ, that is where all obedience ceases.' During the whole time no Quarterly Conference brought a charge against a Methodist minister for preaching Nazi ideology, and, to my knowledge, not a single Methodist minister has had to go before a denazification tribunal on the charge of having aided the Nazi Party."

In regard to the policy of neutrality adopted by German Methodism, Bishop Sommer said: "We read our Bible and found that we were in the same position as Daniel in Babylon or Jesus Christ or Paul, when he wrote Romans XIII, under the Roman Emperors. The protests that these did not make did not lie in our tradition. We did not see what good it would do. On the other hand, it would certainly have led to the destruction of the Methodist Church in Germany. So, for the very same reason, in order that the Gospel might continue to be preached, in order to keep our churches alive, we did not protest. Logically, whoever blames us for that must blame the men of the underground movement for not coming out into the open to be shot. We never compromised, nor betrayed a Christian principle, but we did want the break to come, if it was to come, on a clear-cut religious, and not a semi-political issue, like Paul in Phil. 1:13."

Because there was no exemption of the clergy from military service, sixty-seven per cent of the Methodist pastors were drafted into the army or navy, and twenty-six preachers and theological students were killed during the war. In addition 1,650 laymen were killed in battle and a considerable number were destroyed by the bombing of the cities.

Much property was also destroyed. Of the 398 church edifices in German Methodism in 1938, 141 were more or less destroyed by 1945. The Publishing House at Bremen was demolished. Ten deaconess hospitals and homes were completely destroyed and nine others were seriously damaged. The Seminary at Frankfurt-am-Main was partially wrecked. A German Methodist committee has estimated the total war damages at more than nine million dollars.

ITALY

Methodism in Italy during World War II suffered from the financial restrictions placed upon it by the Fascist regime. No funds could be sent by the English Methodists after June, 1940, and all the properties of the former Methodist Episcopal Church in Italy were sequestered. The preachers and their families suffered much from lack of financial support, and the retired preachers and widows were especially in difficult circumstances. In April, 1945, some of the superannuated pastors and dependent widows were receiving as little as four dollars per month.

When the war came to Italian soil Methodist property suffered. The Casa Materna Orphanage at Portici, near Naples, was damaged by bombing and by the occupation of troops. The church and parsonage at La Spezia were completely destroyed, and seven other churches in northern Italy were seriously damaged.

The outstanding feature, however, of Italian Methodism was its participation in the resistance movement against Fascism and Nazism. The pastor at Alessandria, Ariele Chiara, because of his anti-Fascist activities, had to go into exile. At Genova-Sestri, pastor Alfredo Scorsonelli and many of his members were Partisans, and those captured were deported to Germany. Francesco Leali, the pastor at Milan, was imprisoned for his Partisan activities, and Anziano Guiseppi, the leader of the Italian Methodist youth movement, was an outstanding Partisan. Another Methodist youth, Marco Buson, a student at the University of Milan, was killed for his anti-Fascist underground work. The Methodist Church on Via Firenze, at Rome, was a center of anti-Fascism before and during the war. The pastor, Anselmo Ammenti, used the church as a hiding place for people trying to escape from the Fascists and Nazis, and at one time there were seventy-eight refugees secreted in the church.

AUSTRIA

Methodism also suffered much in Austria during World War II. Superintendent Hinrich Bargmann wrote in 1945: "Nearly every man was ordered to the army and our daughters had to work for the armament factories and the mothers and their little ones had to leave for fear of bombardment." There was surveillance of Methodist leaders by the Gestapo. There was also much destruction of Methodist property. The First Methodist Church and the

Second Methodist Church in Vienna were damaged by bombs, while another church in Vienna was completely destroyed.

YUGOSLAVIA

During part of the war period the Yugoslav Provisional Annual Conference ceased to exist. When Hungary took over Northern Yugoslavia in 1940, Methodism in that section became a part of the Hungarian Provisional Annual Conference. In like manner, when Bulgaria conquered southern Yugoslavia, the supervision of the Methodists in Macedonia was assumed by the Bulgarian Methodist superintendent. The former Yugoslav superintendent, George Sebele, became during several years of the war a district superintendent in Hungarian Methodism.

HUNGARY

Hungary, as a Nazi satellite country, suffered through the invasion and conquest by the Russian armies. During the struggle much Methodist property was destroyed and damaged. Some of the buildings of the Methodist Social Center at Budakesci were looted by both the German and Russian soldiers. Normal church activities almost ceased during the last year of the war. From December, 1944, until June, 1946, Russian soldiers were billeted in the home of Janos Tessenyi, the Methodist superintendent, and he was for several months practically a slave laborer for the Russians.

BULGARIA

Bulgarian Methodism was also affected by the participation of Bulgaria in World War II as a Nazi satellite. When Bulgaria declared war on America, the Methodist properties were placed under government control. Funds for salaries were not available and the superintendent, Alfons Pratsch, advised the preachers to secure secular employment. Although retaining their pastorates, they became lecturers, farmers, colporteurs, accountants and laborers in factories. Only one of the congregations, the Central Church in Sofia, was able to support a pastor.

The work of the American School for Girls at Lovetch was greatly hampered. On October 5, 1942, the Bulgarian Nazi regime removed the school from Methodist auspices and it became a school of modern languages under government control. The two missionaries, Miss Mellony Turner and Miss Ruth Carhart, were permitted to remain for a short period as teachers of English, but during the latter part of the war they were placed under semi-internment.

CZECHOSLOVAKIA

The European Methodists who suffered most during the war were those of the nations occupied by the Nazi armies. Czechoslovakia experienced the longest period of suffering, being for six long years under Nazi control.

When the Germans entered Czechoslovakia they immediately began an attack upon Methodism, because Czechoslovak Methodists prior to the war had been outspoken in their opposition to Nazism. The preachers were forbidden to use any biblical materials which clashed with Nazi doctrines. The Methodist hymnals were censored, and such hymns as "Faith of Our Fathers," "The John Huss Hymn," "Forward, Forward at the King's Command," and all hymns that referred to Jesus Christ as Lord or leader of mankind were deleted by the Gestapo. Upon the creation of the Nazi puppet state of Slovakia in 1939, under Monsignor Tiso, all Methodist churches were closed in Slovakia.

The Methodist superintendent, Dr. J. P. Bartak, being an American citizen, was not molested until Germany declared war on America, but on that same day he was arrested and placed in a concentration camp. Later he was released in exchange for German prisoners in America.

The successor of Dr. Bartak as superintendent was Vaclav Vancura, a Czechoslovak citizen. After he had preached in Prague on the text, "For one is your Master, even Christ, and all ye are brethren," he was seized by the Gestapo. He was told that Adolf

Hitler, not Jesus Christ, was his master, and that all men are not brethren, for the Czechs were to be the slaves of the Master Race. Vancura was beaten, some of his teeth were knocked out, he was forbidden to preach again in Prague, and he had to report each week to the Gestapo.

Other preachers and laymen suffered in a similiar manner. Ladislav Schneider, pastor of the Central Church at Prague, was imprisoned by the Nazis, and when released he weighed only eighty-two pounds. Many laymen died in concentration and slave labor camps.

Some Methodist property was destroyed in Czechoslovakia. A few churches were damaged by bombs, artillery fire, and misuse by the armies. Bombs dropped near the headquarters building in Prague and wrecked the interior. The orphanage at Tynec was used alternately by the German, American, and Russian armies and it suffered much abuse.

Czechoslovak Methodists were prominent in the underground movement against Nazism. The leader for Czechoslovak freedom at Velvary was the Methodist preacher, Josef Koucurek. This young pastor rendered such a remarkable service that after Czechoslovak liberation in 1945, despite his protest, the people of Velvary elected him as their first mayor. At Budejovice, the Methodist pastor, Vaclav Hunaty, was such a tower of strength to the Czechoslovak people during the Nazi Occupation that after liberation the city presented the Methodists with a house as a token of appreciation. Superintendent Vancura has stated that every Methodist preacher in Czechoslovakia was a member of anti-Nazi societies, and "as far as I know, none of our full-fledged members betrayed his country or his church during the Occupation, no matter what temptation or pressure came upon him."

BELGIUM

The period from the Nazi invasion of Belgium in 1940 until liberation in 1945 has been well described by A. Parmentier, a Belgian Methodist pastor: "Cinq années de guerre; cinq années

de destruction; cinq années de misère; cinq années de désolation;"
five years of war, destruction, misery, and desolation.

To escape arrest and death by the Nazis, Superintendent
W. G. Thonger and other pastors were forced to go into exile.
Dr. Thonger and his family found refuge in the Ardèche mountains
of France, where for three years he and his family were under the
constant surveillance of the police. W. G. Wilmot went to England,
and Jan Mietes fled to the Dutch West Indies. But other pastors
were not so fortunate. H. H. Stanley was for nearly two years in
a concentration camp, while Robert Van Goethem was imprisoned
twice by the Nazis during the war.

One Methodist pastor, Henri Van Oest, died as a martyr. He
was pastor at Liège, and when the Nazi army entered that city,
Van Oest spoke to his young people on the topic: "The Cross of
Christ versus the Crooked Cross." He was arrested by the Gestapo
and sentenced to five years of hard labor in the Siegberg prison in
Germany, where he died shortly before the prison was taken by
the American army.

Belgian Methodist laymen suffered similarly. Many were sent
to slave labor and concentration camps while some were executed.
Dr. W. G. Thonger declares that it is impossible to exaggerate the
brutality and ruthlessness of the Nazi oppression of the Belgian
people.

Methodist property also suffered. Four churches were completely
destroyed, while seven churches, twelve other buildings, and the
Orphanage at Brussels were seriously damaged. In the destruction
of the Herstal Church and parsonage by a Nazi "buzz-bomb," the
small son of the pastor, Robert Pierre, was killed and Mrs. Pierre
was seriously wounded.

During these difficult years Belgian Methodism was fortunate
in having the leadership of William Thomas. Because of his Swiss
citizenship, Thomas was able to remain at his post as district
superintendent, and he guided all phases of the Belgian work when
so many other leaders were in exile or imprisoned. He was ably
assisted by his wife and Miss Annie Van Groningen, the secretary
of the Belgian Mission since 1922.

POLAND

No other nation suffered as did Poland from the Nazi aggression. Seven million Poles were murdered and six million were sent as slave laborers to Germany. It is estimated that three million Polish Jews were killed during the Nazi Occupation; in May, 1945, there remained only eighty thousand Jews in Poland. At the close of the war there were more than one million orphans in a population of twenty-two million. When the Nazis finally evacuated Warsaw, they so systematically destroyed the city that ninety per cent of the capital was in ruins.

Polish Methodist missionaries suffered along with the other patriots. In December, 1939, Dr. Edmund Chambers, who is a Canadian, was arrested and for five years he was a prisoner in Nazi concentration camps. In December, 1941, another missionary, Superintendent Gaither P. Warfield, and in December, 1942, Miss Ruth Lawrence, were placed in internment camps, but these were later exchanged for German civilians in America.

The Polish pastors were also mistreated. Thomas Gamble, seventy years of age, was sent with his wife to internment camps for two years. Another pastor, Joseph Naumiuk, and his wife were forced into slave labor. Superintendent Konstanty Najder and his wife were exiled from Warsaw. The suffering of the Polish Methodist pastors can be illustrated by an incident at the Polish Annual Conference held at Katowice in July, 1946. This was the first session of the Conference after the close of the war. The roll of the pastors was called alphabetically, and six of the first seven to report had either been in a concentration camp, in prison, or a slave laborer. The Methodist laymen suffered in a similar manner.

Much Methodist property was damaged or destroyed. The seven-story headquarters building on Mokotowska Street, Warsaw, was gutted. During the Warsaw insurrection it was on the front line of fighting. After the surrender of the Polish patriots in October, 1944, the building was dynamited and burned by the Nazis, and at the close of the war only two rooms in the great building could be used. All other Methodist property in Warsaw was completely destroyed and Methodist buildings in Poznan, Grudziaz and Danzig were damaged.

NORWAY

During the Nazi Occupation of Norway five Methodist churches were destroyed, as was the Old Folk's Home at Vadso. Churches and chapels were requisitioned by the Nazis and used as military barracks, so that in northern Norway only two Methodist churches were available for services. Even the Children's Home in Tromso was taken by the German army. Several preachers and many laymen were sent to Nazi concentration camps, while others to save their lives fled to Sweden and England. Bishop Theodor Arvidson states: "Not one of our preachers, and practically none of our members, were lured to serve the interests of the Occupation powers and in every movement that was made in the name of the Christian faith and Christian principles of life, the Methodist Church was at the front and partook openly and in an outspoken way."

The experiences of the Norwegian Methodist Publishing House are typical of the sufferings under Nazi Occupation. The Nazis required Eilert Bernhardt, editor of *Kristelig Tidende,* to submit all manuscripts to three different Nazi agencies prior to publication. A greeting from a Norwegian Methodist missionary abroad was, for example, deleted. The editor was charged by the Gestapo with being an accomplice of a foreign bishop, and he dared not refer to Bishop Raymond J. Wade. The editor later explained: "For that reason it happened once that we desired to extend a greeting from Bishop Wade, and we found it most expedient to greet from *Brother* Wade—amazing to a good many people. We did not think it advisable to endanger ourselves and the paper for the sake of a title." Again the editor has stated: "But what rendered editorial work particularly trying during this period is the fact that we were not able to write according to the dictates of conscience and our Christian point of view. We were obliged to remain dumb spectators to all the revolting injustice which had been reigning. That brought us untold grievance and pain." The Nazis tried in vain to force the editor to publish propaganda articles regarding alleged terrible conditions in democratic countries and glorifying the alleged improvements in Norway after the arrival of the Nazis.

After 1942 the Nazis forbade the further publication of books by the Norwegian Methodist Publishing House and all books in stock were censored. When it was found that the Norwegian translation of *The Choice Before Us,* by Dr. E. Stanley Jones, contained a criticism of Nazism, all copies of the book were ordered confiscated. A Nazi official, with a revolver pointed at the editor, said: "As from this moment your life is the price if one single copy of Jones's book is sold. Have you understood?" The editor replied that he understood, but after the war ended he told how he evaded the ruling: "A gang of Germans now started carrying the books away, while I tried to put aside as many copies as I could. And they were quite a few. These copies I have not sold, but still they circulated freely during these years, either as gifts or loans, and perhaps some took books without my permission."

DENMARK

In regard to Denmark, Bishop Theodor Arvidson writes: "In Denmark the Methodist Church did publicly protest against the persecution of the Jews and the police officers. There was not one Methodist minister who showed any degree of Nazi sympathy. Not one member of the Methodist Church has been accused as being against the interest of the country. The members partook in the underground movement against the Occupation. In one church, which had one hundred and ninety members, two men were sent to the concentration camps in Germany, three had to flee to Sweden, three had to disappear in the home country and hide themselves and two were killed by the Germans in the street." Two churches on the island of Bornhalm and part of the Central Mission Building in Copenhagen were destroyed during the war.

FINLAND

Finland suffered much during World War II, having been twice invaded by Russia and also having German soldiers on her soil.

The final treaty with Russia deprived Finland of one-tenth of her territory and one-fourth of her industries.

Finnish Methodism also suffered during the war period. Sixty per cent of the Finnish-speaking Methodists lived in the territory ceded to Russia, and they thereby lost their homes and were scattered to other parts of Finland. Through bombings and loss of land to Russia, Methodism lost its largest congregation at Vuoksenlaakso, two churches and a deaconess home at Viipuri, a church at Koivisto, and an orphanage at Hango. The Methodist property loss was estimated at twenty-five million Finnish marks, with only one-tenth of the loss being reimbursed by the government.

THE BALTIC STATES

The Methodists in the Baltic States of Estonia, Latvia and Lithuania have been described as having "suffered indescribably" during World War II. In 1940 these three Baltic nations, as a result of an agreement between Russia and Germany, were absorbed by force into the Soviet Union. Many Methodist preachers and laymen went underground to avoid military or forced labor service for the Russians. In June, 1941, Germany invaded the Baltic States and drove out the Russian army. One Methodist said: "We greeted the Germans as liberators but found the same harsh treatment as under the Russians." In October, 1944, the Russians reoccupied the Baltic States and thousands of the Baltic people were forced to accompany the retreating German army, later becoming Displaced Persons in Germany. Some were able to find refuge in Sweden. In 1949 there are still sixty-five thousand Baltic citizens in Displaced Persons Camps in Germany, while in Sweden there are twenty-seven thousand Estonians. There were many Methodists among these. In 1945 there were twenty-three Baltic Methodist refugee preachers in Displaced Persons Camps in Germany. Some of these later were able to go to America, where they are now serving as pastors.

World War II practically destroyed Methodism in the Baltic States, for these former independent countries are now an integral part of the Soviet Union. The few remaining Methodists suffer under the anti-religious policy of Russia, but it is reported that some laymen still hold religious services in parts of the former Baltic States. Bishop Theodor Arvidson has been advised not to visit this area lest his presence might cause further persecution of the few remaining Baltic Methodists.

SWITZERLAND

Switzerland, as in World War I, was able to remain neutral in World War II, but the country was soon surrounded by belligerent nations and the Swiss Methodists were cut off from their brethren in America. As one pastor stated it: "No papers, no books, no letters came in." No bishop was able to reach Switzerland, and Dr. Ferdinand Sigg, publishing agent and editor of *Der Schweizer Evangelist* of Zurich, served from 1941 to 1945 as president of the Switzerland Annual Conference and rendered unique and faithful service.

Although Switzerland was neutral, the nation was under military mobilization, which involved at one time twenty per cent of the entire male population. This absence of laymen handicapped the normal program of Methodism. As early as 1939 there were only three male employees of the normal number of fourteen left in the Methodist Publishing House at Zurich. Deaconesses were also called into special military hospital service. The high cost of living especially affected the pastors.

Despite this situation much progress was made, particularly in institutional activities. The Deaconess Society acquired a Tubercular Sanatorium in Davos, a clinic in Lucerne, and a Rest Home at Gais. In the beautiful Bernese mountains at Reuti-Hasleberg there was founded "Victoria," a resort home for Bible schools, missionary meetings and youth conferences.

SWEDEN

Although Sweden was a neutral nation, the Methodists, as well as other religious groups, were affected by the war. Many laymen and young preachers were called into military service. The cost of living increased to such an extent that it seriously lowered the income of the churches. In 1941 it was reported that many of the pastors were in financial distress, since the war had caused a complete breakdown in the finances of the local churches.

Although financially handicapped, the Swedish Methodists sacrificially endeavored to help Methodists who were suffering under Nazi control in Norway and Denmark and under Russian domination in Finland and the Baltic States. They joined with other Swedes in caring for the refugees that came from these occupied countries. Fifty thousand Finnish children were given refuge in Sweden. The Swedish Methodists sent food and clothing to the Methodists in adjoining countries. Even during the Nazi Occupation of Norway they sent a wooden chapel and parsonage to the Methodist congregation at Kristiansund, Norway.

SPAIN

Spain was nominally a neutral country during World War II, but there is no doubt that Dictator Franco did all in his power to assist the Fascists and Nazis. Persecution of the remaining Methodists in Spain continued, and at the close of the war few Methodists were to be found anywhere in Spain.

ATTITUDE TOWARD PERSECUTED JEWISH PEOPLE

It shall ever be to the honor of the European Methodists that they did not fall victims to the anti-Semitism of Nazism, but became the protectors of the Jewish people even at personal risk of imprisonment or loss of life. This was true in all parts of European Methodism. Concerning Germany, Bishop J. W. E. Sommer wrote: "I helped a number of Jews to get out of Germany. Most of our ministers did similar things. It was risky, but we could see some good coming out of it." The Methodist church on Via Firenze, in Rome, was a center of refuge for persecuted Jews, and many were given shelter and false identity cards. Charles Lutz, a Swiss Methodist layman, while serving during the war as Swiss consul as Budapest, Hungary, saved the lives of sixty thousand persecuted Jews of that country. In Sweden the Methodists gave assistance to many Jews who escaped from Germany.

In the Nazi-occupied countries the persecuted Methodists became the special protectors of the Jewish people. Bishop Theodor Arvidson states that "it is significant that when anti-Semitic regulations were made by the Nazi government in Norway, the first public meeting of protest was held in the Central Methodist Church at Oslo." In Denmark the Methodists publicly protested against the persecution of the Jews. One reason for the harsh persecution of Belgian Methodists was because they had given assistance to Jewish refugees escaping from Germany. Twenty Jewish children were hidden in the Methodist Orphanage at Brussels during the entire period of the war. In Czechoslovakia, Superintendent Vaclav Vancura and his Methodist colleagues saved the lives of many Jews by hiding them and then later sending them secretly to England. At the Polish Annual Conference of 1946 a Polish Jew publicly thanked the Methodists of Poland for helping the Jews during those years when three million Polish Jews were killed by the Nazis.

One of the martyrs of European Methodism during World War II was Helen Stranska, a young, beautiful and brilliant Jewish girl, who while studying in Prague became a member of the Vrsovice Methodist Church. When the war began she was seized by the Gestapo and was sent to the Nazi concentration camp at Oswiecim, Poland, where she was murdered. During the period of mistreatment prior to her execution, she wrote the following poem, which she entitled "NEVER":

> "Go on and beat me, beat me, if you will,
> My hand is helpless.
> That inward beauty and invisible within me,
> You cannot crush by means at your disposal.
> And if you beat me in the head,
> And if you smash my heart,
>   Remember,

> That more there is to me
> Than body's carnal crust.
> I have a soul that never,
> No, never, will give consent
> To thoughts of malice.
> And since my heart with love doth overflow,
> No enemy, no death,
> Can crush my soul."

Commenting upon this poem, Dr. J. P. Bartak, superintendent of Czechoslovak Methodism, made the following appropriate statement: "Such were the sentiments of this beautiful character. She died a veritable martyr to the cause. And I submit that no matter how discouraging may be our statistics, and no matter how hopeless the material and moral damage caused by the disaster through which we have passed, there is hope for a Church in which souls are converted, in which souls are inspired to express genuine Christian sentiments in words and deeds, that is still producing martyrs as in the days of early Christianity, men and women who with their last breath testify to their loyalty to our Lord and Saviour, Jesus Christ, and stake their all on our Master's thesis, that the force by which this world is to be subdued ultimately is not material but spiritual, not atomic energy, but loving hearts, or as the late president of the Czechoslovak Republic, Thomas Garrigue Masaryk, expressed it: 'Not Caesar, but Christ.' "

DISCUSSION SUGGESTIONS

1. Discuss the general effect of World War II on the Methodist churches in Europe: (1) in the Nazi-controlled countries; (2) in the Allied nations; (3) in the neutral countries.

2. Cite examples of the persecution and suffering of Methodists in Belgium, Poland, Czechoslovakia, Italy and other countries.

3. From the facts set forth in this chapter is there any evidence that the Methodists "sat on the sidelines or went over to the Nazis" during World War II?

CHAPTER VI

METHODISM SINCE 1945

WORLD WAR II was a "total war," and the Methodists suffered with the other citizens of the European nations. Many members and adherents were killed on battlefields and in concentration camps or were victims of the bombing of cities. At least one-fifth of the Methodist property in the belligerent countries was destroyed. The Methodists in the neutral nations of Sweden, Switzerland and Spain were indirectly affected by the war.

The vitality of Methodism was shown by the rapid post-war recovery of most of the national groups. The author had the privilege of visiting many of the European Methodists shortly after the close of the war, and he was amazed at the optimistic spirit of these weary and suffering Christians. He often stated in articles and addresses: "I have found hungry, poorly clad, sick and penniless Methodists, but I have not found discouraged Methodists." The Church not only survived World War II, but many leaders had constructive plans in May, 1945, for reconstruction and expansion.

The churches were encouraged in these tasks by the American, Swiss, Swedish and British Methodists. The Methodist Committee for Overseas Relief was created by the General Conference of 1940 as the official relief agency of American Methodism, and under the wise leadership of Bishop Herbert Welch and Bishop Titus Lowe the group expended between 1940 and 1949 more than $8,000,000. It is the unanimous verdict of the European Methodist leaders that this rendered a most efficient and humanitarian service, and many persons are living today only because of the money, food, medicine and clothing made available by the Committee.

Other agencies rendered similar assistance. The Swedish, Swiss and British Methodists organized relief committees, and some help was also available through the World Council of Churches. Thousands of relief packages were also sent direct by American Methodists to Europe.

At the General Conference of 1944, held one year before the close of World War II in Europe, the Crusade for Christ was authorized. One phase of the Crusade was the raising of more than twenty-seven million dollars for relief and reconstruction in war-torn countries and the strengthening of Methodist institutions at home and abroad. Funds for immediate relief and reconstruction in Europe were therefore available when the hostilities ceased, and Crusade appropriations made possible the partial reconstruction of damaged and destroyed properties. The Crusade also provided for the education in America of many young European Methodists.

In many ways the European Methodists have made phenomenal progress since the close of the war, as the following brief accounts will indicate.

SCANDINAVIAN COUNTRIES

A progressive policy has characterized Scandinavian Methodism since 1945. The Northern Europe Central Conference was held at Gothenburg, Sweden, in April, 1946. Theodor Arvidson of the Sweden Annual Conference was elected bishop. Another session of the Northern Europe Central Conference was held at Bergen, Norway, in September, 1948.

The Swedish Methodists continued the relief program which was started during the war. Liberal collections of funds and relief supplies were made in the local churches, and shipments of Swedish products brought help to thousands of people in Finland, Norway, Poland, Denmark and Germany. One preacher, Gideon Henriksson, was released from certain pastoral duties, in order to serve as director of the Swedish Methodist relief program.

The Norwegian and Danish Methodists were for a short period after May, 1945, themselves in need of relief, but by 1947 they had sufficiently recovered and were able to send aid to the more needy people of Europe. The Norwegian Methodists by that date were sending relief supplies to Finland and Poland, and the Danish Methodists joined with other churches in assisting the thousands of German refugees in Denmark.

There has been much progress in the rebuilding of damaged and destroyed Methodist property. Crusade for Christ appropriations were made for restoring in Norway the churches at Molde, Bodo, Hammerfest and Kristiansund and the Old Folk's Home at Vadso. In Denmark Crusade funds helped to liquidate debts, rebuild the destroyed Danish Methodist Publishing House, and repair the great Jerusalem Church in Copenhagen. Pressing financial obligations of Finnish Methodism were also met through Crusade for Christ grants.

The most striking feature of Scandinavian Methodism since 1945 has been in the field of foreign missions. Many young people volunteered for foreign service. Ingvar Haddal, secretary of the Norway Annual Conference, declared in 1949: "We have so many candidates that according to simple arithmetic it would seem impossible to send all of them out. Many of them have the best education this country can offer. Here the world-wide Methodism must help us." Although there are only one thousand members in the Finland-Swedish Provisional Annual Conference, yet six of them were commissioned in 1947 as foreign missionaries. These Finnish Methodists had suffered much during the war, but they assumed the full support of one of their missionaries, while the Methodist Youth Fellowship prepared to support another one of the group. There are (1949) nearly one hundred Scandinavian Methodists serving as foreign missionaries.

Another evidence of the vitality of Scandinavian Methodism is the large number of volunteers for the ministry, especially in Norway. There are thirty-three students in the Union Scandinavian School of Theology, of which twenty-two are Norwegian Methodists. The active Methodist Youth Fellowships account for most of the volunteers in Scandinavian Methodism for Christian service.

There are (1949) nearly 28,000 Methodists in the Stockholm Area, divided as follows: Sweden, 11,600; Norway 8,600; Denmark 3,300; Finland 2,100; Baltic refugees 2,000.

SWITZERLAND

Before World War II had ended the Swiss Methodists had organized a Methodist Relief Society. Under the leadership of Superintendent Erwin Muller and Dr. Ferdinand Sigg, a sacrificial relief program was promoted by the pastors and local churches. The proximity of Germany made possible the immediate sending of supplies to German Methodists, and soon similar assistance was available for the Austrian and Hungarian Methodists. Refugee children were welcomed into the homes of the Swiss Methodists, and pastors from Germany, Belgium and Austria were given vacations in Switzerland.

The publishing interests of Swiss Methodism, under the guidance of Dr. Ferdinand Sigg, have been expanded since 1945. There are, in addition to the Publishing House at Zurich, six Methodist bookstores in Switzerland, and six periodicals are sponsored by the Swiss Methodists. *Der Schweizer Evangelist* has a weekly circulation of more than five thousand copies, which is remarkable in view of the fact there are only twelve thousand Methodists in Switzerland. The Swiss have made a valuable contribution by providing literature for German Methodists, whose publication facilities were destroyed during the war.

There has been an increased interest in foreign missionary work on the part of the Swiss Methodists. In addition to their missionaries in the Balkans, China and Singapore, they sent two new missionaries in 1947 to North Africa and one in 1948 to India. Other young people are now preparing for future missionary service in North Africa.

Swiss Methodists are encouraged by the number of candidates for the ministry and other forms of Christian service. There are ten Swiss Methodist theological students. Prior to World War II the students were trained at the Theological Seminary at Frankfurt-am-Main, Germany. During the war period they were sent to the Basle Mission Seminary, but it has become possible to resume the former relation with the seminary at Frankfurt-am-Main.

Swiss Methodism is self-supporting and has not received any

of the Crusade for Christ funds. It should be remembered, however, that the churches are self-supporting only because of the sacrificial spirit of the pastors and their families. The uniform salary for preachers is very low and the post-war high cost of living has made it very difficult for the pastors to live upon their small salaries.

GERMANY

The German Methodists began in 1945 to rebuild their destroyed and damaged properties. A donation of $500,000 from the Crusade for Christ gave assistance and encouragement in this task, and by 1948 the local congregations in Germany had raised an additional quarter of a million dollars for reconstruction purposes.

Relief assistance was sent by the Methodist Committee for Overseas Relief, the Swiss, Swedish, and British Methodists and the World Council of Churches. The German Methodists organized their own relief committee, and Bishop J. W. E. Sommer says, "from our poverty we collected money and supplies, such as clothes, potatoes, fruit and furniture, and distributed them."

As early as November, 1946, it was possible to hold a session of the Germany Central Conference, with delegates present from all the Occupation Zones. Dr. J. W. E. Sommer was elected bishop and a constructive program was adopted. A second session of the German Central Conference was held at Frankfurt-am-Main in October, 1948. All the delegates from the five annual conferences of Germany were present at the General Conference of 1948.

Despite much destruction and damage of Methodist deaconess properties, the deaconess movement has expanded since 1945. In 1947 thirty thousand patients were cared for by the deaconesses in Methodist hospitals. Bishop Sommer wrote in 1948: "In addition, a large number of deaconesses are engaged in other hospitals, in private nursing, or in social work of various kinds. During the last year our deaconesses have had 250,000 persons under their care."

When the war ended there was only one student in the Methodist Theological Seminary at Frankfurt-am-Main and the property had been damaged. The buildings were repaired and during the academic session of 1948-1949 there were thirty-two students, of which three were Swiss. Bishop Sommer states: "We could have had three times as many if we had not kept our standards very high."

Evangelism has characterized post-war German Methodism. The year 1947 has been described as probably the year of greatest advance in the history of Methodism in Germany. By 1948 there was a ten per cent gain in membership. There are (1949) sixty-two thousand Methodists in Germany.

Much progress has been made in Sunday School and youth activities. In 1948 Bishop Sommer reported: "Our Sunday School work is progressing with leaps and bounds, so that, in some cases, we have to introduce two successive houses, as the moving-pictures do." As to the youth program Bishop Sommer stated: "In our youth work we have a strong ecumenical trend, frequently meeting with the young people of other churches. We are particularly anxious to draw into this fellowship young people who are entirely outside the Church and the belief in God."

The State Churches of Germany have adopted since 1945 a different policy toward the Methodists and have for the first time officially recognized the Methodists and other Free Churches on an equal basis with the State Churches. The Free Church leaders were invited in March, 1948, to meet with official representatives of the State Churches. One result was the founding of the Co-operative Fellowship of Christian Churches in Germany. Its aims are to promote the ecumenical movement both within and outside of Germany. Dr. Martin Niemoeller was elected president and Bishop J. W. E. Sommer was chosen vice-president.

POLAND

Methodism made much progress in post-war Poland. The membership has increased from one thousand in 1939 to fifteen thousand in 1949, and the pastoral charges in the Polish Provisional Annual Conference increased from twenty to fifty-three. In October, 1947, a new Methodist theological seminary was dedicated in Warsaw, and it had thirty students during the academic session of 1948-1949. Crusade for Christ funds made possible the repairing of the great headquarters building in Warsaw, and there was reopened in 1946 the Methodist English Language School, which had an enrollment in 1949 of seventeen hundred students.

A number of reasons explain this unprecedented recovery and growth. Methodism in Poland was built upon strong foundations, with emphasis upon evangelism. The loyalty and suffering of the Methodists during the Nazi Occupation made an indelible impression upon the Polish people. The post-war Polish government in 1945 annulled the concordat with the Vatican, and through the separation of Church and State promised equal treatment for all religious groups. In November, 1945, Methodism was granted official recognition for the first time in Poland.

In 1945 a new field of service for Methodism was opened in the former East Prussia, now a part of Poland. As a result of the evacuation of East Prussia by the Germans there were hundreds of abandoned Protestant church buildings. The withdrawal of the German members left only a small group of Polish Protestants in these parishes, and they lacked spiritual supervision, since all the pastors had returned to Germany. To save Protestantism in this area it was necessary for the stronger Polish Protestant Churches to provide pastoral supervision. The Polish government offered to assign the abandoned church buildings to the various denominations if they could furnish pastors. An agreement was made between Bishop Jan Szeruda of the Lutheran Church and Superintendent Konstanty Najder of the Methodist Church, and approved by the Polish Ecumenical Committee, which provided that the Methodists should work in the northern section and the Lutherans in the southern part of former East Prussia, now known as the Mazury District of Poland. A district of Polish Methodism has been organized in this new Polish territory.

The laws of Poland require that the leaders of all Polish churches must be Polish citizens. Because of this legislation all places of official leadership in Polish Methodism were assigned in March, 1949, to native Polish pastors and laymen.

ITALY

Constructive steps were taken by the Italian Methodists at the close of the war, the most important being the union of the two Methodist groups. This was accomplished by May, 1946, when all the congregations formerly sponsored and supported by the American and British Methodists merged to form the Methodist Church of Italy. Emanuele Sbaffi became the first superintendent of united Italian Methodism. There are in Italian Methodism about five thousands members, with thirty-two ordained preachers and fifty local preachers.

Generous donations from the Crusade for Christ reconstruction funds made possible the repairing of Casa Materna, the Italian Methodist orphanage, which continues its work of serving three hundred orphans. A statement by an UNRRA official in 1946, contrasting Casa Materna with the average Italian orphanage, is very illuminating. He wrote as follows: "Just previous to our visit to Casa Materna, we were out at Aversa looking over a Provincial Orphanage for Boys. The need of physical equipment was very obvious, but even more striking was the educational philosophy and regimentation behind the whole project. The marching, stolid, expressionless, and sameness of pattern in which the one hundred and sixty boys lived was sickening. By contrast it was like coming from sorrow to joy, from death to life, when we went from Aversa to Casa Materna. The attitude, conduct, freedom, and joy of the children was so obvious that one could not help seeing the difference between life based on a vital religion and life hanging helplessly on."

The future of any Protestant group in Italy will be affected by the attitude of the Italian government, for without religious freedom Protestantism will face many difficulties. Despite the protest of liberal Italian political leaders, the new constitution adopted in March, 1947, included the Lateran Pact and the

Concordat of 1929. Thus the religious settlement, with all its anti-Protestant features, made between Mussolini and the Vatican was carried over into post-war Italy. The basic complaint by the non-Roman Catholics of Italy is that these parts of the Italian constitution have established a virtual Roman Catholic monopoly over the spiritual life of the nation.

Belgium

Belgian Methodism is a striking example of remarkable vitality, for it has made a rapid recovery from the effects of the Nazi Occupation. Through Crusade for Christ funds some of the Methodist properties were restored. A gift of Mrs. J. B. Fleet, of Greensboro, North Carolina, as a memorial to her nephew, Charles Benjamin Pickard, an American soldier who died in the liberation of Belgium, made possible the rebuilding of the destroyed church at Herstal, and gifts secured by Dr. Kenneth W. Pope, while pastor of the First Methodist Church at Austin, Texas, provided a new church building at Ypres.

Although there are only five thousand members and adherents in Belgium, the Methodist Church is wielding an influence far out of proportion to its numerical strength. It is recognized as one of the three major Protestant groups in the country. In 1947 there was an increase of fifteen per cent in membership. Dr. W. G. Thonger wrote in 1947: "The evangelical churches in Belgium confront possibilities of conquest such as we have never known in this little land since the far-off days of the Reformation. It is our conviction that The Methodist Church is particularly equipped to face this situation. This is clearly demonstrated by the place which it occupies today in the life of Belgian Protestantism and the consideration it receives in official circles in spite of its relatively small numerical strength."

Since 1945 there has been a renewed interest in missionary work in the Belgian Congo. One pastor and one local preacher of Belgian Methodism are serving as Protestant chaplains in the

Congo. In April, 1949, two Belgian Methodists went as missionaries to the Congo while others are preparing for service in that field.

CZECHOSLOVAKIA

With the evacuation of Czechoslovakia by the German armies in the spring of 1945 the four thousand Czechoslovak Methodists began a phenomenal recovery. At the Annual Conference of 1946 one preacher was appointed as Conference evangelist to organize Methodist societies among the people who were transferring to new homes in Czechoslovakia. New Methodist churches were organized, notably at Karlovy Vary. In 1947 Dr. J. P. Bartak could state that, although there had been no mass evangelistic movement, "there had been genuine conversions and signs of the awakening zeal for Christ and the spreading of His Kingdom."

Since the close of the war there has been a remarkable youth movement in Czechoslovakia. Copying the program of the American Methodist Youth Caravans, young Czechoslovak Methodists visited various cities and held evangelistic meetings. Many young people volunteered for full-time Christian service. There are (1949) five Methodist students enrolled in the John Huss Faculty (the theological department of the University of Prague) and two are preparing in American universities for the ministry.

The best example, however, of the spirit of post-war Czechoslovak Methodism was the assuming in 1947 of a Missionary Special in North Africa. In May, 1945, the Czechoslovak Methodists were bankrupt, hungry, and lacked decent clothing. Two years later the Woman's Society of Christian Service decided to help the Methodist missionary program in North Africa. Even in their poverty, the Czechoslovak Methodists never lost their world vision and are now doing their part in helping the needy people of North Africa.

AUSTRIA

The close of World War II made possible the recreation of a separate Austrian Mission Conference. After the invasion of

Austria by the Nazis in 1938, and its inclusion in the Third Reich,
the old Austrian Mission Conference had been incorporated into the
Southeastern Germany Annual Conference.

In May, 1945, Hinrich Bargmann resumed the superintendency
of the Austrian Mission Conference. He and the Austrian Methodists found themselves, however, in a peculiar situation. All the
former Austrian Methodist property had been listed after 1938 as
belonging to the Methodist Church in Germany, and in 1945 it was
considered by the Occupation authorities as enemy property. Since
1945 there has been a custodian for this church property, but the
Methodists have been granted the use of the buildings for religious
purposes. Being assured by the Allied authorities and the Austrian
government that the properties will be returned to Austrian Methodists after a peace treaty has been signed, steps have been taken
to repair much of the property. In this the members were helped
by a grant from the Crusade for Christ reconstruction funds.

Since 1945 much progress has been made in Austria. There was
a twenty per cent gain in membership in 1947. As in the past the
number of adherents far exceeds the membership, which is only
fifteen hundred. The Austrian Methodists have rendered a valuable
contribution in caring for many displaced persons and refugees who
have come into Austria from other countries.

YUGOSLAVIA

In Yugoslavia, Hungary, Bulgaria and Spain, Methodism has
been unable to make the rapid recovery which has characterized the
other Methodist groups in Europe since 1945.

The close of World War II found Methodism in a very
precarious position in northern Yugoslavia, for the majority of
the members had been of German background. Many of them left
with the retreating German armies, while those who remained were
placed in concentration camps. All German-speaking congregations
of all denominations were closed. Some of the churches were
damaged or destroyed during the war. The Methodist Sanatorium
at Novi Sad was requisitioned in 1945 by the Yugoslav govern-

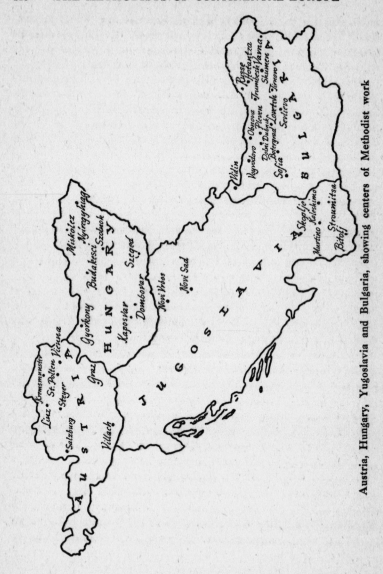

Austria, Hungary, Yugoslavia and Bulgaria, showing centers of Methodist work

ment, and it is still (1949) being used as a national tubercular hospital. Since 1946 George Sebele has been the only Methodist preacher stationed in northern Yugoslavia, and he has endeavored to serve the few Methodists still living in that area.

The Methodist churches in the Macedonian section of southern Yugoslavia were not so adversely affected by the war as were those of the north. They are, however, located in a region now in dispute between Bulgaria, Yugoslavia and Greece. Some of the pastors in southern Yugoslavia are growing old and there are as yet no recruits to take their places. The properties are in great need of repair, since no funds have been available since 1939 for the upkeep of the churches and parsonages. It is estimated that there are about one thousand members in Yugoslavia.

HUNGARY

World War II and its aftermath seriously affected Hungary. By the forced migration of Germans and Slovakians two-thirds of the Methodists left Hungary shortly after the close of the war. Only one thousand remained, these being of Hungarian nationality.

The financial condition of post-war Hungarian Methodism became desperate. Formerly there had been an income from the rent of apartments in the headquarters building in Budapest and from fees from the sanatorium at Budakesci. The loss of rents through increased taxation, the decreased work at the sanatorium, plus the economic inflation, destroyed almost all of these sources of income. The orphanage at Budakesci had to be closed, and Superintendent Janos Tessanyi said: "We could no longer see the children die of suffering both cold and hunger." In 1948 the highest salary paid in Hungarian Methodism was $56 per month, while eight supply pastors were receiving only $13 per month.

Communist control of the Hungarian government brought additional difficulties to the Methodists. Although the Methodist Church was for the first time officially recognized in Hungary in November, 1947, this was followed two months later by the arrest of several Methodist preachers. To escape the treatment meted out to other Hungarian church leaders in recent months the Methodist superintendent was forced to flee. The sanatorium at Budakesci has been taken over by the government and Methodist officials have been replaced by Communist agents.

BULGARIA

With the Russian occupation of Bulgaria and the overthrow of the Nazi government in September, 1944, the three thousand Methodists were placed in jeopardy because of the former close relations of Bulgarian Methodism with Germany. For twenty years the Methodist superintendent had been a German citizen and many of the pastors were educated in Germany. Because they had accepted employment with German commercial agencies in Bulgaria during the war period, two Bulgarian Methodist pastors were arrested in 1944. One was acquitted but the second was sentenced to life imprisonment, later lowered by amnesties to seven years.

For a few years the new Bulgarian government seemed to be tolerant toward the Methodists. Two months after the overthrow of the Nazi government, Miss Mellony Turner was given permission to reopen the American School for Girls at Lovetch. It soon had the largest enrollment in its history, having for the academic session of 1947-1948 ten applications for each vacancy. It was even possible to offer elective courses in the Bible.

Although the post-war Bulgarian constitution guaranteed religious freedom, in 1948 the Communist government suddenly began a systematic attack upon Protestantism. One of the first acts was to abolish all "foreign" schools. Despite the protests of the parents of the students, the American School for Girls at Lovetch was closed in July, 1948. Fifteen Protestant preachers, including Superintendent Yanko N. Ivanoff and two other Methodist preachers, were arrested, and while the charges were treason and similar crimes, the basic reason for the arrests was the refusal of the Methodists to endorse the Communist regime. Superintendent Ivanoff was sentenced in March, 1949, to life imprisonment while the two other preachers were given lesser sentences.

The policy of the Communist regime in Bulgaria is shown by the enactment of a recent law which forbids all Bulgarian churches to have any relationship to foreign churches. No Bulgarian church leader can even correspond with religious organizations, church officials or institutions outside of Bulgaria except by permission of the Bulgarian Minister of Foreign Affairs. All pastors must be approved by the state. No church can maintain hospitals, orphanages or similar institutions and can have no work for young people. The Communist regime apparently is satisfied with the policy of the Orthodox Church in Bulgaria, for it has been promised financial support by the government and the Minister of Cults has described the Orthodox Church as the traditional religion of the Bulgarian people "and in form, spirit and meaning a people's democratic Church."

SPAIN

There has been no change since the close of World War II in the intolerant policy of Dictator Franco toward the Protestants. The few Protestants in Spain live under restrictions and suffer persecution. They must send their children to schools where the Roman Catholic religion is taught to all pupils, and they cannot publish their own literature, since all religious publications in Spain must bear the Roman Catholic imprimatur. According to a decree of 1945 Protestants may hold worship services "provided they are held within buildings and with no public manifestation." Only members may attend. If one person should be found by the police at such a service without a card of membership, the entire congregation could be arrested for proselyting. Protestants experience difficulty in securing buildings in which to worship, because recent attacks have made owners afraid to rent property to Protestants. After a visit to Spain in the summer of 1948, Dr. John Sutherland Bonnell, pastor of the Fifth Avenue Presbyterian Church of New York City, declared that the "saddest spot in Europe with respect to religious freedom is Spain." He further stated: "As a Protestant clergyman, I would prefer today to be preaching in Prague, behind the 'iron curtain' than in any city of Spain "

There are no Methodist preachers in Spain. Most of the laymen are also in exile. The Model School at Alicante is still used by agencies of the Franco regime.

SOME PROBLEMS

The foregoing constitutes an account of European Methodism as of August, 1949. The author realizes that readers will be interested in the future, but it is hardly possible to prophesy concerning the future of any phase of European life. A few observations, based upon personal experiences and many conferences with European Methodist leaders, are offered as to the problems and prospects of Methodism in Europe.

Among the most difficult problems is the growth of Communism in post-war Europe. At this time (August, 1949) militant Communism is in control of the governments of Albania, Bulgaria, Czechoslovakia, Hungary, Poland, Roumania, Russia and Yugoslavia.

Although differing in minor details within countries, there has been a Communist pattern in regard to churches. Upon its increase in power after the close of World War II, Communism promised religious freedom, and clauses guaranteeing the same were inserted into the new constitutions. There usually followed a few years without interference with the churches. Unbiased observers have admitted that for a time after the close of World War II there was even more freedom of religion in certain European countries dominated by Communists than under the pre-war reactionary regimes. It was hoped that this policy would be permanent.

Communism, however, like Nazism and Fascism, is a totalitarian system in which individuals and churches are required to be subservient to the state. It has been found that religious freedom, as written into the constitutions of Communist-dominated countries, limits religious activities to a very narrow field. The normal youth programs of churches are blocked because the Communist state assumes responsibility for the total education of the young people.

Attempts are made to confine religious activity to formal worship services. Thus far the Communists have not attempted to destroy the churches, but rather to control them and make them tools of the state. The trend is to require the establishment of national churches and to break all ties with churches in other countries, especially with those in Western nations.

Because of the international and world-wide nature of Methodism, our members are looked upon with suspicion by the Communist leaders. Attempts are being made to compel the Methodists to disavow any organic relation with Methodists in other nations. Pressure is also brought to bear upon the churches to endorse the Communist regime.

Methodists in America should understand the serious difficulties faced by their brethren in Communist countries. It may be necessary, because of threats or even force, to set up autonomous Methodist churches in certain European nations. Severe persecution has already come to some European Methodists, notably in Bulgaria, because of their refusal to endorse the Communist program. Methodists in Europe will not approve Communism or any similar totalitarian systems, and the result may be that the churches in some countries will be closed and the leaders imprisoned or exiled. The author has no doubt, however, that despite this persecution there will always remain a remnant of faithful Methodists in each country, worshipping in secret and facing persecution as did the Christians of the totalitarian Roman Empire. It should also be remembered that persecution is not new to the European Methodists.

A second problem for European Methodists is the difficulties which they face from other types of totalitarian regimes which are linked with ecclesiastical intolerance. Spain is now the best example of such difficulties. Roman Catholic leaders in Spain publicly proclaim their hostile attitude toward Protestants. F. Cavelli, a Spanish Jesuit, gave the official position of Spanish Roman Catholicism when he wrote on April 3, 1948: "The Catholic Church, being convinced by reason of her divine prerogatives that she is the only true church, claims for herself alone the right to freedom, for this right may only be possessed by truth and never by error." Because of this combination of Roman Catholic intolerance and Franco totalitarianism the future for Methodism or any Protestant group in Spain is not bright.

Italian Methodists are also alarmed by statements emanating from the Vatican. On September 18, 1947, *L'Osservatore Romano,* the official Vatican newspaper, declared in an editorial: "Historically and socially it is absurd to consider all religions equal in all countries. . . . It would be strange if a religion professed by one million people should be judged equal to another professed by forty million. . . . In all manifestations of social and political life the equality of religion and cults is an absurdity." The position stated by Pope Pius XI on May 30, 1929, was again endorsed, namely: "In a Catholic state, liberty of conscience and liberty of discussion are to be understood and practised in accordance with Catholic doctrines and Catholic laws."

Secularism is a third ism that faces Methodism in Europe, as well as in other parts of the world. The naïve optimism that a revival of religion would sweep over Europe because of the human suffering during World War II has proved an illusion. World War II did not change people reared under the pre-war totalitarian systems which substituted the state for God. Secularism and materialism in Europe are in many ways more powerful today than was the paganism faced by the early Christians in the Roman Empire.

Another tragic fact is that the inhumane spirit of pre-war totalitarianism did not cease with the close of armed hostilities in Europe. There are still concentration camps, and men and women are yet held in slave labor. Anti-Semitism has not disappeared. The end of the war did not stop the military spirit of some European nations. Enmity between certain national groups has even been deepened by the war.

It will require the total resources of all Christians in Europe, plus assistance from their brethren abroad, to meet and conquer these irreligious trends now so prevalent. The Methodists of Europe, although small in number, can make a valuable contribution in this united effort.

A changed Europe or a changed world will come only through people whose hearts and intellects have been transformed through personal contact with divine resources. Reliance cannot be placed upon nominal membership in churches, for in State Church theory all citizens are members of a church, but such church allegiance has proved very ineffective in meeting the problems of modern Europe.

SOME CONTRIBUTIONS

Methodism in Europe will continue, as in the past, to insist that Christians must demonstrate their religion by the living of changed lives. Bishop John L. Nuelsen always said, in referring to the European Methodists : "They are hand picked. They are Methodists not in consequence of any decree of civil law. They are members of the Methodist Church because each one decided to join the Methodist Church of his own free-will."

Attendance at worship services is a good example at this point. Visitors to Europe often remark upon the small attendance in the great cathedrals, but they fail to visit the Methodist chapels, where the attendance is very high. Bishop J. W. E. Sommer gives the following report concerning church attendance at Stuttgart, Germany, in 1947 : "In greater Stuttgart, where the State Church is particularly strong and active, it has 150,000 members, while the Methodist Church has 1,500. The average attendance, however, in the former is 9,200, a little more than 6% ; in the latter it is 1,400, or more than 90%." Bishop Sommer adds : "It is, therefore, probably an understatement to say that 75% of the members of the State Church are religiously indifferent or opposed to the Christian faith."

The Methodists of Europe are rendering a contribution through their evangelical agencies such as the Sunday School, the use of laymen, evangelism, and youth activities, many of which have been adopted by the State Churches. This represents one of the influences of Methodism upon Protestantism in Europe. In regard to this Bishop Sommer writes : "In the first place, very much of what is religiously vital in the State Church goes back directly or indirectly to Methodist influences. A State Churchman, Professor Christlieb advised his co-denominationalists to combat Methodism by making it superfluous through adopting the good it brought. His advice has been followed to a certain extent, but there is no question that only the existence of a strong Free Church by the side of the State Church can keep these tendencies alive." Methodism will continue, as in the past, to be the means of salvation to many Europeans who will never become Methodists. Because of this it has often been asserted, as the historian Green declared of the early Wesleyans, that the Methodist Church itself is the smallest result of the Methodist movement in Europe.

Although it is often overlooked, the Methodists of Europe are contributing much to the ecumenical movement. They have never attacked other religious groups. Bishop Nuelsen declared in 1939: "Far from assuming an attitude of superior piety and looking down upon other churches, the Methodists gratefully acknowledge the works of faith and labours of love accomplished by the established churches. They have been ready ever since the days of Wesley, and they are so at the present time, 'to form a league defensive and offensive with every soldier of Jesus Christ.' "

It is easy for European Methodists to be ecumenical, for they have always been members of an international and world-wide church. This has given them the vision of an ecumenical church that knows no national boundaries. It has been more difficult for the leaders of the Protestant State Churches of Europe to comprehend the true meaning of ecumenicity because of their heritage of a church connected with a particular state, which has produced national churches. Too often their conception of ecumenicity has been that of fraternal relations between State Churches, and not the larger view of ecumenicity between all Christian groups, whether State Churches or Free Churches, whether large or small.

The greatest contribution, however, that can be made by the European Methodists is to continue to champion the principle of the Free Church. After nearly five years of residence in Europe, the author is convinced that the union of church and state is responsible for many of the problems of European society. There is much truth in the statement made in 1947 by Dr. Stanley Struber,

Chairman of the Baptist World Alliance Commission on Religious Freedom, namely: "The battle for religious freedom will be a long and hard one. It must be fought not merely within the nations and governments but within religion itself. Our experience in Europe taught us that complete freedom is yet to be won for the so-called Free Churches in countries dominated by the state-church system. A State Church which violates the very principle of democracy is in a poor position to lead Europe into a new era of liberty and religious freedom. Moreover, a church which receives financial aid from the government cannot be absolutely free. And the Christian Church must, above all else, be free if it is to champion the causes which will set Europe free, morally and spiritually."

The Methodist Church must continue to insist on the separation of church and state, and to hold that church membership must be based upon personal decision. The recent political developments in some nations of Europe make clear the absurdity of the continued union of church and state. It is an anomaly for a Christian church to receive financial aid from Communist and other totalitarian governments. As long as churches in Europe are affiliated with the state, there is great need for European Methodists to present the claims and virtues of a Free Church.

There are many prophets of gloom concerning European Christianity, and there are many discouraging reports about Europe and its churches. The author has noted, however, that this pessimism comes from "religious observers" who make brief visits to Europe, rather than from those persons who week after week carry on the duties of parish work. American pastors who visit Europe usually return home with a conviction that European culture and religion can be rebuilt. They understand from personal experience that religious work anywhere is hard, and that extreme difficulties often bring the noblest eras in Christian history.

Methodists must take the historical perspective. Civilization will not disappear because there has been a major catastrophe in Europe, and because Communism is temporarily threatening our conception of society. Modern Methodists should be true followers of John

Wesley. Two hundred years ago English religious leaders were declaring that Europe was in the evening of the world, and even Wesley admitted that ungodliness was the universal characteristic. That however, did not deter Wesley from launching in that great crisis an evangelical movement that brought hope, comfort and courage to many people. In like manner, any religious group that renders faithful service to the European people will have a following. Methodists in all parts of the world should assist the European Methodists as they, though hampered by losses during and since World War II, accept the challenge of secularism, materialism and all forms of totalitarianism. The Advance for Christ and His Church provides during the quadrennium (1948-1952) a specific way in which this assistance can be rendered.

DISCUSSION SUGGESTIONS

1. Country by country, review the progress of Methodism, in reconstruction and evangelism, since World War II.

2. Discuss Methodism "behind the Iron Curtain" on the basis of the facts set forth in this chapter and what you have learned from other sources.

3. What are some of the present problems of European Methodism? What are some of its contributions?

4. Discuss the principle of a Free Church, and its values as compared with the State Church idea.